ALASTAIR SAWDAY'S
SPECIAL PLACES TO STAY

MOUNTAINS
OF EUROPE
SKI CHALETS, HOTELS AND B&BS

Contents

ALASTAIR SAWDAY'S
SPECIAL PLACES TO STAY

£12.99/$19.95

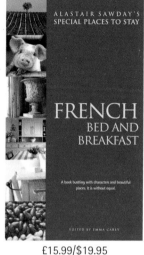

£15.99/$19.95

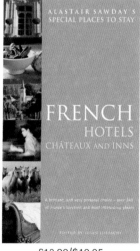

£13.99/$19.95

£11.99/$17.95

Credit card orders (free p&p) 01275 464891
www.specialplacestostay.com

In US: credit card orders (800) 243-0495, 9am–5pm EST,
24-hour fax (800) 820-2329 www.globepequot.com

First edition
Copyright © 2004 Alastair Sawday
Publishing Co. Ltd
Published in October 2004
Alastair Sawday Publishing Co. Ltd
The Home Farm Stables, Barrow
Gurney, Bristol BS48 3RW
Tel: +44 (0)1275 464891
Fax: +44 (0)1275 464887
E-mail: info@specialplacestostay.com
Web: www.specialplacestostay.com

The Globe Pequot Press
P.O. Box 480, Guilford,
Connecticut 06437, USA
Tel: +1 203 458 4500
Fax: +1 203 458 4601
E-mail: info@globe-pequot.com
Web: www.globepequot.com

Design:
Caroline King

Maps & Mapping:
Bartholomew Mapping, a division of
HarperCollins, Glasgow

Printing:
Pims, UK

UK Distribution:
Penguin UK, 80 Strand, London

US Distribution:
The Globe Pequot Press, Guilford,
Connecticut

ISBN 1-901970-45-0

Printed in UK

Back
Page

Photo opposite Nick Woodford

ASP - who are we?

We began by chance, in 1993, seeking a job for a friend. On my desk was a file: a miscellany of handsome old houses in France, some that could provide a bed, and some a meal, to strangers.

I ran a small travel company at the time, taking people off the beaten track; these places were our 'finds'. No chain hotels for us, no tourist restaurants if we could possibly visit old manor houses, farms and châteaux whose owners would breathe new life into our enthusiasm for France.

So Jane set off with a file under her arm and began to turn it into a book. We were then innocent enough to ignore advice and print 'far too many' - 10,000. We sold them all, in six months - and a publishing company was born.

We exhorted readers to enjoy a 'warm welcome, wooden beams, stone walls, good coffee' and nailed our colours firmly to the mast: 'We are not impressed by TVs, mini-bars and trouser-presses'. We urged people to enjoy simplicity and authenticity and railed against the iniquities of corporate travel. Little has changed.

Although there are now more than 25 of us working out here in our rural idyll, publishing about 20 books, we are holding tightly to our original ethos and gradually developing it. Our first priority is to publish the best books in our field and to nourish a reputation for integrity. It is critically important that readers trust our judgement.

Our next priority is to sell them - fortunately they sell themselves, too, such is their reputation for reliability and for providing travellers with memorable experiences and friendships.

However, publishing and selling books is not enough. It raises other questions: what is our impact on the world around us? How do we treat ourselves and other people? Is not a company just people working together with a shared focus? So we have begun to consider our responses to those questions and thus have generated our Ethical Policy.

There is little intrinsically ethical about publishing travel guides, but there are ways in which we can improve. Firstly, we use recycled paper and seek the most eco-friendly printing methods. Secondly, we are promoting local economies and encouraging good work. We seek beauty and are providing an alternative to the corporate culture that has done so much damage. Thirdly, we celebrate the use of locally-sourced and organic food among our owners and have launched a pilot Fine Breakfast scheme in our British B&B guide.

But the way we function as a company matters too. We treat each other with respect and affection. An easy-going but demanding office atmosphere seems to work for us. But for these things to survive we need to engage all the staff, so we are split into three teams: the Green team, the Better Business team and the Charitable Trust team.

Each team meets monthly to advise the company. The Green team uses our annual Environmental Audit as a text and monitors progress. The Better Business team ponders ethical issues such as flexible working, time off in lieu/overtime, and other matters that need a deep airing before decisions are made. The Trust team allocates the small sum that the company gives each year to charities, and raises extra money.

A few examples of our approach to company life: we compost our waste, recycle the recyclable, run a shared car to work, run a car on LPG and as another on a mix of recycled cooking oil and diesel, operate a communal organic food ordering system, use organic or local food for our own events, take part in Bike to Work day, use a 'green' electricity supplier, partially bank with Triodos

Photo opposite: Paul Groom

(the ethical bank in Bristol), have a health insurance scheme that encourages alternative therapies, and sequester our carbon emissions.

Especially exciting for us is an imminent move to our own eco offices; they will conserve energy and use little of it. But I have left to the end any mention of our most tangible effort in the ethical field: our Fragile Earth series of books. There are The Little Food Book, The Little Earth Book and The Little Money Book – hugely respected and selling solidly – look out for new titles in the Fragile Earth series.

Perhaps the most vital element in our growing Ethical Policy is the sense of engagement that we all have. It is not only stimulating to be trying to do the right thing, but it is an important perspective for us all at work. And that can only help us to continue to produce beautiful books.

Alastair Sawday

Acknowledgements

Nick Woodford came to us with the idea for this book. We were so impressed by his sheer 'chutzpa' that we said "yes" – and don't regret it. For Nick has done all the promotion, all the research and all the foot-slogging. His devotion to the pursuit of special places is rooted in years of work as a 'contractor' for travel companies, negotiating with ski hotels. After all that, he wanted to focus on the places that he loved but could never include in a ski 'package'. Here they are, many of them.

Putting together the first edition of a book like this can be lonely, dispiriting and exhausting. Glamorous and exotic it is not; the deep beds and the cheese fondues are, at best, only a respite. But Nick slogged on – and on. He wrestled with an unfamiliar database and a tight administrative system, and he has produced a splendid book. We, and anyone who goes to the mountains to walk or to ski, owe him our gratitude.

We also owe much to Roanne Finch, the office 'anchor' for the project, and to Jo Boissevain, our in-house writer. Both have helped create this book.

Alastair Sawday

Series Editor
Alastair Sawday

Editor
Nick Woodford

Editorial Director
Annie Shillito

Managing Editor
Jackie King

Production Manager
Julia Richardson

Web & IT
Russell Wilkinson, Matt Kenefick

Copy Editor
Jo Boissevain

Editorial
Roanne Finch, Danielle Williams

Production
Rachel Coe, Paul Groom,
Allys Williams

Accounts
Sheila Clifton, Bridget Bishop,
Christine Buxton, Jenny Purdy,
Sandra Hassell

Sales & Marketing & PR
Siobhan Flynn, Paula Brown,
Sarah Bolton

Writing
Jo Boissevain, Nick Woodford

Inspections
Nick Woodford

Thank you Mum and Dad for your constant support. Thanks, Emily Bradney, for your hard work and thank you to Anne Woodford for helping me get the project off the ground. NW

My first visit to the mountains was a cold one, by early-morning train into the Alps. I slept on the luggage rack, cousins, uncle and aunt on seats and other racks. We were awoken by the bellow of the station master rather than by our alarm clocks, with only two minutes to disgorge. Out went the women, in their nighties, to receive the luggage hastily shoved through the windows by the pyjama-clad males. Two minutes were barely ample for the women and luggage, and not enough for us. We waved forlorn goodbyes.

The train crept through the dawn to the next station where we pattered across the snowy platform in our slippers, to the warmth of the station-master's office. And there we stayed for some hours, awaiting the next train back to our womenfolk and luggage. It was an a rum start to a skiing holiday.

I also remember a ski-lift closing for lunch just as we arrived, our picnic lunch waiting at the top. It is a long way up a mountain with skis on your back and ski-boots on your feet. Could these two incidents occur these days? If not, there are surely other pitfalls. Certainly finding yourself in a grim, cramped and soul-less hotel is still a possibility – and here is a book to help you avoid it.

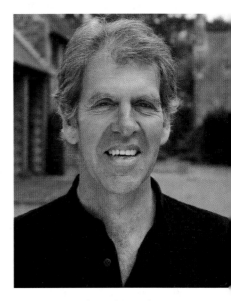

All the reasons for which we began to publish these guides apply in equal measure to this one: to sleep in the wrong place can ruin a holiday. So these wonderful places are chosen for their human warmth and individuality, as well as for their style and beauty. Use the book as a basic planning tool – and build your ski-ing and hiking plans around the places you stay. You will be nourished and exhilarated by them.

Alastair Sawday

Photo above: Paul Groom

Introduction

CHOOSE YOUR SPECIAL PLACE AND DO YOUR OWN THING...

The Alps and Dolomites stretch 1,000 miles across six countries, from the French Riviera to Slovenia. Never have their snow-capped peaks been so seductive or so accessible – although they have been attracting skiers for 90-odd years, and walkers for even longer. Now everyone can be in on the secret – mountains are addictive things.

Seriously sporty alpinists are spoiled in summer with hiking, cycling and paragliding, mountain-stream swimming, white-water rafting, riding and fishing. And in winter with downhill skiing, cross-country skiing, snowboarding, sledging, skating, curling and snowshoeing.

Photo above Mike Richardson
Photo opposite Nick Woodford

As for the incurably idle, they too can experience bliss – in fresh air, with a glass of genepi and the scent of pine on a warm spring day.

Researching this book has had its ups and downs. I have scaled peaks, plumbed valleys and negotiated thousands of bends looking for these special places. It makes a difference where you lay your head; such things can make or break a holiday. One wintery evening I found myself sheltering from a blizzard in a barn, my car with a flat tyre. Two hours later I arrived dispirited and dishevelled with straw in my hair at the guesthouse I was due to visit. Jurg and Sibylla would have been forgiven for thinking I'd gone round one bend too many, but they beckoned me in, pressed upon me a towel for my hair, a deep armchair and a steaming mug of cocoa. Such simple acts of kindness can be what make a holiday memorable.

For the independent traveller organising a family ski trip six months in advance – or a group of friends taking off for a spontaneous weekend cycling in the mountains – this book is a godsend. Why be bound by the rigid itineraries set by tour operators? Just pick up

Introduction

this guide, choose your special place and do your own thing. Some of our guesthouses, chalets and hotels are well-known, others far less so or not at all; we have panned through hundreds of 'possibles', seeking out owners who share our enthusiasm for authenticity, genuine hospitality and real food. Here you will also find scenery, history, architecture and beds on a heroic scale.

What is a special place?

We are highly subjective in our choices. 'Special' for us is not only about comfort but also about those less obvious things that make a place 'work': originality, generosity, a genuine smile, a fabulous setting. Home-baked bread and a bowl of sweetpeas from the garden can be more enchanting than snazzy toiletries and jacuzzis, however welcome those may be (and this book has its fair share of bubbling hot tubs on sheltered terraces). So, this is a very personal range of places to lay your head – each judged on its merits, and all good value for money.

Villages and Resorts

Some of the best skiing is to be found in the high-altitude, purpose-built resorts that mushroomed in the 60s and 70s. However, these usually lack charm, so there has been a surge of interest in the farming hamlets of the lower slopes,

unchanged for centuries. Staying in these villages – in new, traditionally constructed buildings, or in sympathetic restorations of old ones – may mean a short drive, or free shuttle, to the lifts each morning. As for nightlife, the big resorts may be jumping with clubs and bars, while the chief excitement of the little place down the road may be its annual boules competition. See 'Read carefully, sleep happily' to find the right special place for you.

Which country?

Wiener schnitzel or coq au vin, raclette or risotto? The geography, food, culture (even the lift-technology) of the big four – Austria, Switzerland, Italy and France – vary considerably. Austria has pretty, low-lying rural villages,

Photo above Tim Brook
Photo opposite Nick Woodford

plenty of gentle slopes and breathtaking scenery. France's resorts can be utilitarian, yet are often snow-sure with hundreds of kilometres of challenging piste. Italy's Dolomites have spectacular rock formations rising from the gentle lower slopes, while delicious food and a relaxed way of life guarantee a good time. In Switzerland, everything ticks over with clockwork efficiency – as the cliché has it; the original Alpine destination has masses going for it: spectacular and challenging mountains (more than 100 peaks over 4,000m), immaculate villages and friendly people.

Read carefully, sleep happily

We are here to help you find those places that are right for you. We aim to give honest descriptions of the décor, the setting, the people, the mood. Older places may seem more immediately appealing, but don't overlook the more modern ones – they, too, may have great personality.

Check on anything that is really important to you before confirming your booking. Will the swimming pool be ready by Easter? Will the promised bicycles be shared by others? Does your balcony catch the sun? If 'French antique beds' sound seductively authentic, remember they may be antique sizes, too

(190cm long, 140cm wide) – not good if you were expecting king-size. And if you flee from dining with strangers, a shared chalet or B&B may not be for you.

What you can expect

The variety in this book is impressive: from a deliciously rustic mountain retreat with mains water to a 19th-century villa hung with chandeliers where you can expect flutes of champagne. We don't work with the established 'star' system for it uses criteria different from ours. A hotel we think the world of, for example, may merit a mere two stars because it has no lift. And some owners, unwilling to be swept into a bureaucratic system, refuse to apply for a star rating on principle.

Hotels, pensions and inns

We tend to go for small (or smallish) and independently run hotels. In many of them, however, you can expect all sorts of indulgences: sitting rooms, restaurants and bar, a 'wellness' centre with sauna and spa, a swimming pool indoors or out (or even both), satellite TV, internet and minibar in the bedrooms, bathrobes in the bathrooms and all-day access. At inns, food takes priority over bedrooms, though these will always be decent and clean. And remember, in country areas dinner is often not served before 7.30pm and last orders are rarely taken after nine.

Pensions are more basic, some with no sitting area other than the breakfast room. Many, however, are charming and cosy.

B&B

Our guesthouses and chambres d'hôtes range from the small and intimate to the grand and gracious. Many of our families give you unexpected extras; some will babysit your children, others offer you lifts to the nearest cable car, others rustle up picnics at the drop of a hat. But remember, you are staying in somebody's home, so don't expect room service or breakfast/dinner at a private table. Dinner taken at a communal table, and hosted, can be a wonderful opportunity to get to know your hosts and make new friends. (And if a late arrival is unavoidable, a cold meal may be prepared if advance notice is given.) Owners love guests to stay more than one night, but they may expect you to be out and about until around 4pm. If, however, they are happy for you to be around, check which parts of the house and garden you may use during the day.

Catered chalets

Pure indulgence! Someone to lay on breakfast, afternoon tea, an apéritif and a three- or four-course dinner, wine included, six days a week – and, often, early suppers for children. Some chalets are small and must be booked for a single party during high season; others are

Photo above Hotel de la poste, no 138
Photo opposite Mark Bolton

Introduction

bigger, so you will eat with strangers and make new friends. Catered chalets are a winter thing, with owners and/or chalet staff often willing to help you book ski passes, ski equipment and ski school. Airport transfers may be included in the price. Note that lunches are not, and that chalet staff generally have one night off a week. (Again, check.)

In summer, the majority of catered chalets become holiday homes or B&Bs.

Self-catering

Although there is obviously less of a sense of being looked after in a holiday home, you trade this for the delights of independence and privacy. You can get up and go to bed when you please, prepare your own food, choose your own wine, turn the music up loud (within reason!), give the children the run of the house and garden, nod off with a book by the fire. If it's important to you that your apartment or chalet has a dishwasher/TV/CD-player or wood-burning stove, check with the owners first. Most properties will have a washing machine.

Problems

We only have 200 or so words to tell a story; if you find anything in our books misleading (things do change in the lifetime of a guide), or you think we miss the point, we 'd love

to know. (Perhaps that house with the toys isn't so child-friendly after all.) Please discuss any problem with your hosts at the time; they would be disappointed to discover that you were unhappy and they were not given the opportunity to do something about it.

Mountain food

In the mountains, expect generous portions of diet-defying dishes. Many owners use locally grown ingredients and may well have grown or produced some part of your meal. Breakfasts include coffee and rolls with jams and honey in Austria; sweet pastries in Italy; creamy fruit-based muesli in Switzerland; hot chocolate and croissants in France. And everywhere, except, perhaps, for the more modest places, buffets of fresh and stewed fruits, yogurts, smoked and air-dried meats and local cheeses. At lunch and dinner, many Tyrolean and Savoyard dishes are cooked – by you – at the table: *pierrade*, in which thinly sliced beef or chicken is briefly sizzled on a hot stone; fondue, where cubes of bread are dipped into a pot of hot melted cheese with wine – or cubes of beef into hot oil, then dunked into dips; and raclette: cheese melted under a hot grill and poured, still bubbling, onto steaming new potatoes. (See pages 198-201 for some mouthwatering mountain recipes.)

Bedrooms

We describe them as follows:

double: one double bed

twin: two single beds

twin/double: two single beds that can become a large double

triple or family room: any mix of beds (sometimes sofabeds) for three or more people

suite: either one large room with a sitting area or two or more interconnecting rooms, plus one or more bathrooms

apartment: similar to a suite but generally with an independent entrance and a small kitchen

A twin room is usually larger than a double. Extra beds and cots for children, possibly at extra cost, can often be provided; ask when booking. Where an entry reads e.g. 4 + 2 this means four rooms, plus two apartments for self-catering.

Bathrooms

Assume bedrooms have their own 'en suite' bathrooms; we say if a bedroom has either a separate bathroom or a shared bathroom. For simplicity we refer to 'bath'. This doesn't necessarily mean it has no shower; it could mean a shower only – so check if this is important to you.

Prices

The price range is for two people sharing a room: the lower price is for the least expensive room in low season; the higher price for the most expensive room in high season. If breakfast is not included, we say so and give the price. If there are no single rooms, there will usually be a reduction for single occupancy of a double. During certain high season periods many hotels and guesthouses impose a minimum stay period; these can be from three nights to two weeks – always check.

When prices vary between summer B&B (or self-catering) and winter catered chalet, we give the summer price first.

If half-board is the only option, we give the half-board price, per person (p.p.) per night. Prices for catered chalets and for self-catering are generally per chalet per week.

Photo above Nick Woodford

Introduction

Prices are given for 2004-2005 but cannot be guaranteed so please check when you book and check our web site for up-dates and special offers. Many places offer reductions for longer stays or special prices for children: ask when you book. There is a €/£/$/Swiss franc conversion table at the back of the book.

Lunch and dinner

We say if lunch or dinner is available and give an average price per person. Half-board terms can be good value – and there may be special prices for children. Half-board includes breakfast and dinner; full-board includes all three meals. Prices given are generally per person and include the room. Hotels and inns offer the widest à la carte choice; smaller places may offer a set dinner (at a set time) and you will need to book in advance. In family-run places you may be eating in a separate dining room, served by a member of the family, or with the family itself. Small farms and inns often offer delicious dinners which are excellent value.

Dinner in catered chalets

The number and type of courses you will be offered varies and we have not gone into details, although price may be an indicator. Wine is almost always included, and this can mean a range of things, from a standard quarter-litre carafe per person to a barrel of table wine.

Table d'hôtes

A wonderful opportunity to eat honest, even gourmet, food in an authentic family atmosphere, but don't expect a choice: table d'hôtes means the same food for all and absolutely must be booked ahead. Do specify any particular dietary needs when you book.

Vegetarians and special dietary requirements

In the summer there is normally so much fresh food available that vegetarians should have no difficulty in most areas. Cheeses, yogurt and other dairy products are a significant part of the mountain diet.

Photo above and opposite Nick Woodford

Closed

When closure is given in months, this means for the whole of both months named. So 'Closed: November–March' means closed from 1 November to 31 March.

Symbols

There is an explanation of our symbols on the inside of the back cover. These are intended as a guide rather than as an unequivocal statement of fact; should a place not have the symbol that you're looking for, it's still worth discussing your needs – the owners may be able to help.

Distances to lifts etc

Distances to the nearest pistes or lifts, cross-country trails, lifts for bikes and village centre should be used as a guideline only. Talk to the owners to confirm the best route, and the timings for example of ski buses. The 'closest ski area' is the closest within a 20km or 30-minute drive, and is defined as having 10 or more lifts. Timings to the airport are approximate.

Directions & maps

Look at the map at the front of the book to find your area, then the detailed maps to find the places. The numbers correspond to the entry numbers at the bottom of each page. Or choose from the individual entries, and then check the map

reference at the bottom of the page. Our maps are for guidance only; take a detailed road map to find your way around. Self-catering places are marked in pink on the maps; others are marked in blue.

Practical matters

Telephoning/faxing

International telephone codes

Austria
From UK   00 43 then drop the 0
From US   011 43 then drop the 0

France
From UK   00 33 then drop the 0
From US   011 33 then drop the 0

Italy
From UK   00 39 do NOT drop the 0
From US   011 39 do NOT drop the 0
(except when dialling an Italian mobile phone.)

Photo above Sara Hay
Photo opposite Mark Bolton

Switzerland
From UK   00 41 then drop the 0
From US   011 41 then drop the 0
UK
00 44 then drop the 0
US
00 1 then drop the 0

Phone cards (télécartes, cartes telefoniches) are available in tobacco shops and post offices. There are plenty of telephone boxes, even in the countryside, but most only take cards.

Mobile phones work in most places.

Travel to and from the Alps

Here are some of the options available:

Air travel

There are currently well over 100 flights from the UK to the Alps every day. Greater use of regional airports and low cost airlines means it has never been easier to get there (see the back of the book for major flight routes). However, travelling by air is the least environmentally friendly means of travel. Reduce your impact by visiting www. futureforests.com or www.climatecare.org – see the back of the book for more information.

Going by car

Calais-Geneva is 886km, (a nine-hour drive). There are motorway tolls of approximately €40 each way and a ferry crossing to consider, but, if you have a full car, this may well be the cheapest option. However, a car can be more of a hindrance once you've arrived than a help, particularly in resorts that have strict parking regulations and expensive underground parking.

Going by train

There are two direct services from London to Moutiers or Bourg St Maurice on Eurostar. Both run on a Saturday to coincide with the major tour-operators' changeover day (who also book most of the seats). However, there are also many services that change in Paris. You could consider the Orient Express that passes through St Anton on its way to Venice...!

Airport transfers

Car hire is in most cases the easiest and most economical way of getting from the airport to your destination but do check that there will be parking when you arrive. Baby seats, ski racks and snow chains cost extra and must be booked in advance. Also check that there is a Collision Damage Waiver (CDW) included, or the companies will take a hefty deposit on your credit card.

There are several car-free resorts in the Alps, accessible only by train. In Switzerland the train system is excellent. Times and tickets are available at www.rail.ch – or you can contact the Swiss tourist office. There are special rates for return travel to ski areas and discounts for children under 16. In some cases your luggage can be booked straight through from the departure airport to your hotel room. Amazing! There are also private taxis and shared taxis. Book your taxi ahead to save money. Those waiting at the terminal will charge extortionate amounts for a long journey to the resort. Another option is the shared minibus taxi. There are many firms that pick passengers up from several flights and take them to the resort, making the set fare more affordable for everyone; try www.a-t-s.net. Minibus taxis are normally very efficient, though it may mean having to wait at the airport for other passengers booked on the transfer. Finally, public buses are few and far between so try www. altibus.com for French resorts not served by train.

Driving in the Alps

Having a car in the mountains can give you great freedom and allow you to see places you wouldn't otherwise be able to get to. It can also be essential for shops and lifts in remoter places. However, in some resorts the car can become something of a ball and chain; a constant worry and expense. In high resorts such as Courchevel the police are strict about keeping the roads clear of snow, and if you park illegally you may find your car has been towed away. In some car-free and purpose-built resorts you are obliged to park your car at a fair distance.

In Switzerland and Austria you cannot drive on a motorway without a Vignette, a sticker that is placed on the windscreen, available on the border (Chf45 in Switzerland, €30 in Austria). Check you have anti-freeze and insurance.

Booking

Most places now have web sites and e-mail addresses. We have a booking form at the back of the book and on our web site at www.specialplacestostay. com.

Photo above Tim Brook

But please remember that technology may be put aside at busy times and a small place may just not have the time or the personnel to respond quickly.

Deposits

Some owners ask for a deposit. Where guesthouses don't take credit cards many readers have found it virtually impossible or very expensive to send a deposit by direct transfer, but you can send an ordinary cheque which the owner will bin when you arrive (so no one pays the charges); when you leave, they will ask you for cash for your stay. You may receive a tenancy contract as confirmation. It must be filled in and returned, probably with a deposit, and commits both sides to the arrangement. Failure to stay the full time booked may incur a cancellation charge.

Photo above Tim Brook
Photo opposite Nick Woodford

Paying

Most B&B owners do not take credit cards; check our symbols. Virtually all ATMs (cash machines) in the Alps take Visa and MasterCard. Euro travellers cheques should be accepted; other currency cheques are unpopular because of commission charges. American Express is often accepted in the upper range hotels, Diners Club hardly ever.

Taxe de séjour

In France a small tax that local councils can levy on all visitors may be charged; you may find your bill increased by €0.50-€2 per person per day.

Arriving

Most owners of smaller hotels and B&Bs expect you to arrive between 5pm and 7pm. If you come earlier, rooms may not be ready. If you are going to be late (or early, unavoidably), please telephone.

No-shows

The owners of smaller hotels and B&Bs hope you will treat them as friends by being sensitive and punctual. It's obviously upsetting for them to prepare rooms, even meals, and to wait up late for guests who give no further sign of life. So if you are not going to take up a booking, telephone right away. By the way, there is a tacit agreement among

some B&B owners that no-show + no-call by 8pm, even 6pm in some cases, can be taken as a refusal of the booking and they will re-let the room if another guest turns up.

Seasons & public holidays

It is essential to book well ahead for New Year and February and wise for other months. Be aware of some of the holiday dates that can make booking difficult. (See page185).

Consider taking

- Electrical adaptors: virtually all sockets now have 2-pin plugs that run on 220 / 240 AC voltage
- A universal bath plug in case yours is missing
- Earplugs could be useful for a light sleeper driven mad by the early morning snowplough

Quick reference indices

At the back of the books we direct you to places with rooms at under €100, those with single rooms at under €50, those suitable for children, those within one hour of the airport, those suiteable for people of limited mobility and those within 50m of the piste.

Subscriptions

Owners pay to appear in this guide, though it is not possible for anyone to buy their way in. It would be disastrous for us to allow our standards to be thus undermined. (The fee goes towards heavy compilation and production costs.) We only include places we find special.

Internet

www. specialplacestostay. com

Our web site has online entries for all the places featured here and in our other books, with up-to-date information and direct links to their own e-mail addresses and web sites. You'll find more about the site at the back of this book.

Disclaimer

We make no claims to pure objectivity in choosing our Special Places to Stay. They are here because we like them. Our opinions and tastes are ours alone and this book is a statement of them; we hope that you will share them.

You should know that we do not check such things as fire alarms, swimming pool security or any other regulation with which owners of properties receiving paying guests should comply. This is the responsibility of the owners.

A huge 'Thank You' to those of you who take the trouble to write to us about your experiences good and bad, or to recommend new places. This is how we respond:

- Owners are told about very positive reports.
- Recommendations are followed up with inspection visits where appropriate. If your recommendation leads us to include a place, you receive a free copy of the edition in which that place first appears.
- Poor reports are followed up with the owners : we need to hear both sides of the story. Really bad reports lead to incognito visits, after which we may exclude a place.

We have done our utmost to get our facts right but apologise unreservedly for any mistakes that may have crept in. We would be grateful to hear of any errors that you find. Feedback from you is invaluable and we always act upon comments. With your help and our own inspections we can maintain our reputation for dependability.

And finally

We love your letters and value your comments which make a real contribution to this book, be they on our report form, by letter or by e-mail to info@sawdays.co.uk. Or you can visit our web site and write to us from there.

The mountains can be wild and unpredictable. So go prepared and enjoy them.

Bon Voyage
Happy Travelling!

Nick Woodford

How to use this book

(1) **Rhône Valley-Alps :** Portes du Soleil **(2)**

La Ferme de Nant
La Ville du Nant, 74360 La Chapelle d'Abondance, Haute-Savoie, France

(3) Upstairs is chic and contemporary, downstairs traditional. Susie and Steve have transformed the 1789 farmhouse into a superb chalet that's fully catered in winter. Floor-to-ceiling windows opening to a sunny balcony pull in the views. The open-plan kitchen/living/dining area is vast, with doors off to the bedrooms. Floors are wooden and gleaming, halogen spots illuminate white walls, there's a mix of Savoyard and modern and a giant pop art portrait to add a sparkle. From the first floor you descend the stairs – past a fascinating collection of old wooden sledges that came with the house – to the more traditionally furnished ground floor. This is a delightfully cosy space with an open fireplace in the middle, good new sofas and beautiful country-antique dining room table and chairs. A trap-door leads to a cellar packed with DVDs, yours for winter evenings; the slopey garden has been reshaped to make way for a good-sized, heated pool, open from March. In winter the owners, who live on the top floor with their labrador, can drive you to the pistes. Susie also owns a horse – the riding is wonderful.

rooms	6 doubles/twins. Extra beds. **(4)**
price	B&B €100. Self-catering per week: one floor €1,200; two floors €2,250. Winter: €785-€1,125 p.p. p.w. **(5)**
meals	Dinner €22. Self-catering June-August. Catered in winter. **(6)**
closed	May & October-November. **(7)**
directions	D22 for Chatel; thro' La Chapelle, then left at sign for La Croix. Chalet on 3nd bend. **(8)**

Self-catering/Catered/B&B **(9)**

piste or lift	1km **(10)**	
cross-country trail	1.5km	
lift for bikes	2km	
village centre	1.5km	

	Susie Ward
tel	+44 (0)1872 553055
fax	+44 (0)450 734087
e-mail	susie@susieward.com
web	www.susieward.com

(12) Map 1 Entry 23   **(11)**

explanation

❶ region & **❷** ski region

❸ write up
Write-up, written by us.

❹ rooms
Assume most but not all rooms are en suite; some will have separate or shared bath/shower rooms.

❺ price
The price shown is for one night B&B for two people sharing a room. Half-board prices are per person. Catered/self-catered prices are per chalet per week, unless stated otherwise. A price range incorporates room/seasonal differences.

❻ meals
Prices are per person. If breakfast isn't included we give the price. All other meals must be booked in advance.

❼ closed
When given in months, this means for the whole of the named months and the time in between.

❽ directions
Use as a guide and travel with a good map; the owner can give more details.

❾ type of place
B&B, hotel, catered or self-catered chalet. (Guesthouses, inns and restaurants with rooms come under 'B&B' or 'Hotel').

❿ distance
To nearest piste or lift, cross-country trail, lift for bikes and village centre (in metres and kilometres).

⓫ symbols
see the last page of the book for a fuller explanation:

ⓗ	english spoken		
⚲ wheelchair facilities		good vegetarian dinner options	
🧍 easily accessible bedrooms		guests' pets welcome	
🧒 all children welcome		owners pets live here	
✖ no smoking anywhere		pool	
🗂 credit cards accepted		bikes on the premises	
	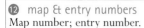	tennis on the premises	

⓬ map & entry numbers
Map number; entry number.

General Map

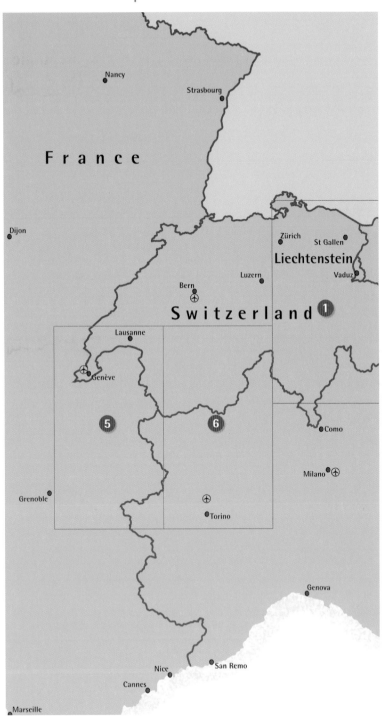

©Bartholomew Ltd, 2004

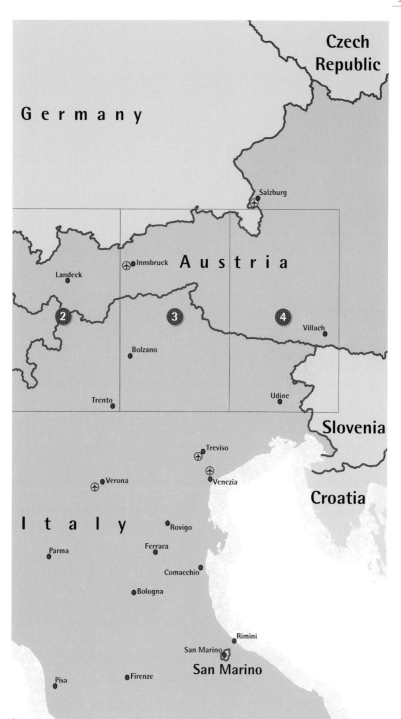

©Bartholomew Ltd, 2004

1: 1,000,000

GERMANY

Schaffhausen
Neuhausen
Rüdlen
Diessenhofen
Stein
am Rhein
Steckborn
Konstanz
Bodensee
Friedrichshafen
96
Eglisau
Henggart
Andelfingen
670
Pfyn
Seerücken
Scherzingen
Märstetten
Weinfelden
Romanshorn
Amriswil
Bregen
Winterthur
Frauenfeld
7
THURGAU
Aadorf
Wil
Rorschach
51
Kloten
Turbenthal
Sirnach
Walisellen
Effretikon
Dübendorf
Flawil
St Gallen
1251
Widnau
Au
Zürich
53
ZÜRICH
Bütschwil
Herisau
APPENZELL
Gais
Altstätten
Hohenem
Uster
Küsnacht
Schnebelhorn
AUSSERRHODEN
Oberriet
Götzis
Thalwil
Meilen
Hinwil 1293
Ebnat-Kappel
Appenzell
APPENZELL
INNERRHODEN
13
AUSTRIA
Horgen
Wädenswil
Stäfa
Rüti
Wald
Kaltbrunn
Nesslau
Feldkirch
VORARLBERG
Satteins
Baar
Zug
Pfäffikon
Jona
Speer
1950
Gams
Nenzing
Bürs
ZUG
Wollerau
Schübelbach
ST GALLEN
Buchs
VADUZ
A14
Unterägeri
Ägerisee
Sihlsee
Einsiedeln
Näfels
Flums
2343
LIECHTENSTEIN
Schesaplana
2965
Arth
SCHWYZ
Wägitaler
See
Glarus
Spitzmeilen
Mels
Bad Ragaz
Rhätikon
Schiers
Gersau
Schwyz
Drusberg
2282
Glärnisch
2501
Pizol
Maienfeld
Zizers
Küblis
Brunnen
Muotathal
2802
GLARUS
Schwanden
Matt
2844
Bauen
2515
Uri-
Rotstock
2928
Altdorf
Bürglen
Erstfeld
Linthal
Elm
Hausstock
3158
Ringelspitz
3247
95
Tamins
Flims
Chur
2533
Hochwang
13
Zizers
URI
Silenen
Oberalpstock
3328
Disentis Muster
SWITZERLAND
Trun
SURSELVA
Domat
Ems
Churwalden
Arosa
Davos
98
99
Wassen
Andermatt
Piz
Medel
3210
Vals
3121
Piz d'Anarosa
3000
Splügen
Cazis
Thusis
Alvaneu
Wiesen
Tiefencastel
Filisur
Zillis
Savognin
Piz
Ela
3339
Bergü
Albula Alpen
GRAUBÜNDEN
Airolo
Ticino
Olivone
Hinterrhein
Rheinwaldhorn
3402
Avers
Piz
Platta
3392
St Moritz
Quinto
Faido
Acquarossa
Bivio
Sils
6
Basodino
3273
Campo
Tencia
3072
Giornico
Mesocco
Campodolcino
Piz
Duan
3131
Lago
da Segl
Peccia
Monte
Zucchero
2736
Biasca
Mera
Bignasco
Cevio
Osogna
2505
Lostallo
Chiavenna
Castasegna
Monte
Disgrazia
3678
TICINO
2322
Maggia
Sasso della
Paglia
2593
Gordona
Samolaco
Bagni di
Masino
Minusio
Gordola
Arbedo
Lago di
Mezzola
Verceia
Dubino
Malesco
Ascona
Locarno
Bellinzona
Gravedona
Adda
Talamona
1962
Cadenazzo
Cavargna
ITALY
PIEMONTE
Maccagno
Porlezza
Monte Legnone
2609
Bellano
Gerola Alta
LOMBARDIA
Foppo

©Bartholomew Ltd, 2004

Map 2

33

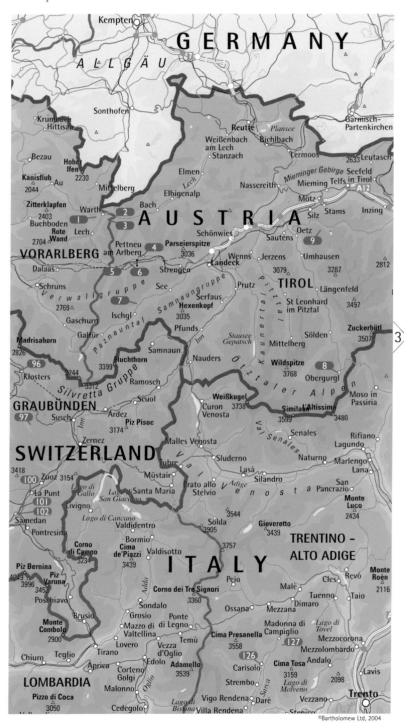

©Bartholomew Ltd, 2004

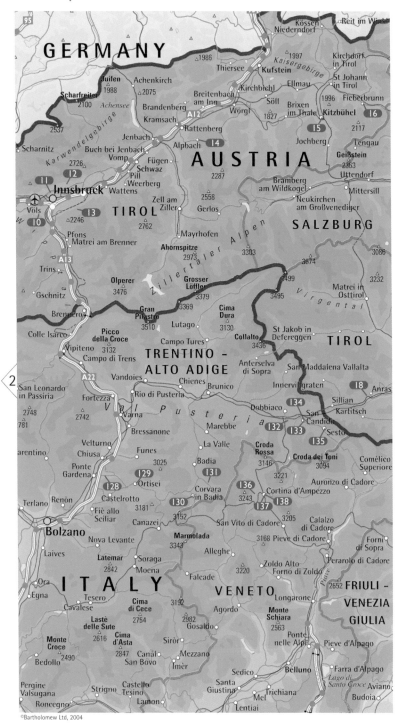

Map 4

35

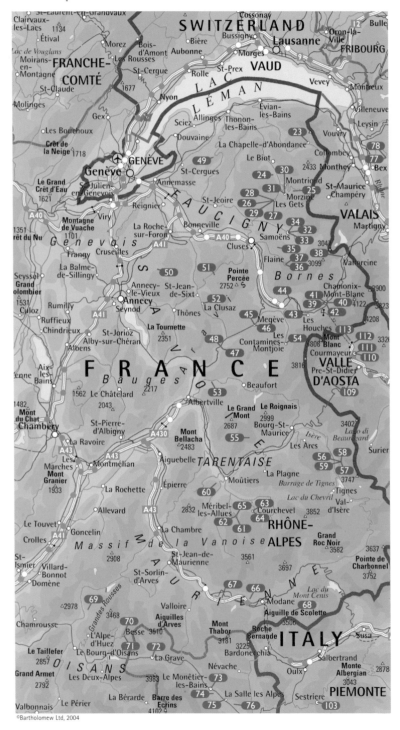

©Bartholomew Ltd, 2004

Map 6

37

Photography by Nick Woodford

austria

Hotel Gasthof Post Lech
6764 Lech, Arlberg, Austria

Small, exquisite, in the family for three generations – the Dutch royals have been fans for years. Even when it was a post office, the Post was a top one: a collection point for the royal mail of the Austro-Hungarian empire. Thanks to smiling Sandra and Florian Moosbrugger and their Tyrolean-dressed staff, the feel is warm and delightful. And this in spite of the super-swish décor, the donning of suits at dinner and the award-studded restaurant that rivals any in this gastronomic village. More Tyrolean perfection in the hunting-style bar with its crackling logs, leather-bound books and mounted antlers, and in the bedrooms, particularly those in the oldest part. Expect floors of wood and seagrass, alpine beds painted red, green and gold, chests and chairs with the patina of age, tiled stoves, embroidered cushions, deep tubs, bowls of fruit. Homemade strudel and jugs of hot chocolate have Lech's sweet tooths beating a path to the front terrace… and the pool and spa are delicious. It's all you'd hope for from the smallest multi-starred hotel in Europe.

rooms	39: 29 twins/doubles, 4 singles, 6 suites.
price	€210–€710. Singles €160–€310. Suites €320–€840.
meals	Dinner €35–€95.
closed	Late April-June; 28 September-28 November.
directions	Exit S16 at St Anton for Flexen Pass & on to Lech. Hotel in village centre, on right.

Hotel

piste or lift	50m		Moosbrugger Family
cross-country trail	150m	tel	+43 (0)5583 2206 0
lift for bikes	150m	fax	+43 (0)5583 2206 23
village centre	10m	e-mail	info@postlech.com
		web	www.postlech.com

Map 2 Entry 1

Hotel Tannbergerhof
6764 Lech, Arlberg, Austria

Lech is Austria's most exclusive resort. And the Wiener family run some rather exclusive places to stay. The Tannberghof is the biggest and most central, a chalet-hotel on the pretty high street that curves beside the river. Its bar and restaurant open to a sprawling sunny terrace – Lech's number one meeting point for skiers. Many of them surface later, dressed for tea dancing and disco. The main lounge is comfortably alpine, with plump cushions around a central stove, warm lighting, pictures, prints and the odd painted chest. Bedrooms have newly panelled ceilings and brand new bathrooms; the à la carte restaurant serves traditional and international dishes at candlelit tables. Down below is a vaulted wellness centre. There's no indoor pool, so hop on the free shuttle and use Chalet Hilde's; this charming old chalet sits the edge of the village, and is neatly divided into apartments. Haus Bernhard (where you can B&B or self-cater) in nearby Stubenbach is cheaper. Because of the resort's controls on parking for day visitors, its pine-sprinkled pistes are rarely crowded.

rooms	30: 25 doubles, 5 suites.
price	Half-board €89–€259 p.p.
meals	Half-board only.
closed	April-May; October-November.
directions	Exit S16 at St Anton for Flexen Pass & on to Lech. Hotel in village centre, on right.

Hotel

	Heller & Karl Wiener	piste or lift	150m
tel	+43 (0)5583 2202/2203	cross–country trail	150m
fax	+43 (0)5583 3313	lift for bikes	500m
e-mail	info@tannbergerhof.com	village centre	10m
web	www.tannbergerhof.com		

Map 2 Entry 2

Gasthof Rote Wand
Zug, 6764 Lech, Arlberg, Austria

No longer does the dear old gasthof sit on its own next to the white chapel with the bulbous spire. There are now at least 20 other chalets in the village, and the third generation of the Walch family has built a swish new extension onto the back, linked by a red passageway. Choose an apartment with a zen-like kitchenette, or cocoon yourself in one of the bedrooms: high-ceilinged, airy, luxurious, with big windows and decked balconies with views. Glass, steel and halogen-sparkle, coupled with pastel colours and minimalist furniture, give the place a snazzy city feel. Throw in a swimming pool, sauna, wellness area and indoor golf and you have a seriously sophisticated set-up. The restaurant, too, is striking, with its modern red pillars and slatted, contoured ceiling; it extends onto a parasoled terrace in spring. The Rote Wand was a 1960s pioneer of Swiss fondue: winter visitors, snug in rugs, used to arrive from Lech by jingling horse-drawn sleigh. They still do (snow permitting!). Outdoor lunches are popular with skiers and the homemade pasta delicious. A glittering hideout.

rooms	26 +1 2: 26 twins/doubles. 12 apartments for 2-3.
price	Half-board €148-€255 p.p.
meals	Half-board only.
closed	May-November.
directions	Exit S16 at St Anton for Flexen Pass & on to Lech; left over bridge to Zug.

Hotel

piste or lift	10m	
cross-country trail	10m	
lift for bikes	3km	
village centre	3km	

		Walch Family
tel		+43 (0)5583 343 50
fax		+43 (0)5583 343 540
e-mail		rotewand@rotewand.com
web		www.rotewand.com

Map 2 Entry 3

Levett Chalets
Nasserein, St Anton, Austria

Two chalets, one roof. And ski school, hiking paths, gondola and Nasserein's bars at your door. The original chalet is a 17th-century farmhouse; its sibling was added in 1995, with a shared sauna and ski room in-between. In the old chalet you have a sitting room with huge charm: a panelled ceiling, white curtains at Alpine windows, pale throws on sofas, striped rugs on boards. Dine by candlelight at a rustic table in the alcove; clamber steep stairs to bed. In New Levett find white walls and blond pine floors, glass-topped tables, halogen lights and a delightfully fresh, Nordic feel. The slopey-ceilinged living room is at the top, making the most of the view, its flamboyant, ceramic woodburner backed up by central heating. Jenni and her team are generous to a fault – there's even a Playstation for kids – and give you cooked breakfasts, tea with homemade cake, and (six days a week) pre-dinner drinks, canapés and four-course dinner with wine. Oh, and a walking guide for two days in the summer. St Anton's star still shines brightly, its nightlife is a 10-minute walk. Superb.

rooms	Old Levett for 8: 2 doubles, 2 twins. New Levett for 16-18: 4 doubles, 4 twins.
price	£349-£939 p.p. per week. Price includes UK flights.
meals	Catered.
closed	26 April-26 June; 19 Sept-14 Dec.
directions	Exit S16 for St Anton; through St Jakob; exit St Anton-Ost; left at top of junc.; immed. right; right again, into Gertrud-Gabl-Weg.
Catered	

	Jenni Lloyd	piste or lift	100m
tel	+44 (0)1449 711952	cross-country trail	300m
fax	+44 (0)1449 711245	lift for bikes	100m
e-mail	info@albustravel.com	village centre	1km
web	www.albustravel.com		

Map 2   Entry 4

Bergschloßl
Kandaharweg 13, 6580 St Anton, Arlberg, Austria

Inn-keeping runs in this family. (One off-shoot owns the illustrious Post in Lech.) Johanna is proud of the tradition and couldn't be nicer. And the position of her small, single-turreted pension couldn't be better: in the middle of celebrated St Anton, pistes and trails at the door. Each bedroom is big, each different, with a fireplace, ceramic stove or a corner kitchen. Most are wooden clad, all are immaculate. Some have the original built-in wardrobes, others are decorated with modern alpine furniture stencilled in red, green and gold. Carved wooden benches, plump cushions, vases of flowers and old-fashioned lights add a glow. Johanna has ensured that bathrooms are bigger than average, and decorated the tiles herself, using traditional glazes from a friend's studio. Breakfasts are Austrian and hearty – local cheeses, hams, fresh juices – accompanied by great views. Ski (or stride) to Lech from the door; swap stories with friends in the Spiegel Bar as darkness falls. Sauna, steam room, 'big Annabelle' and gym soothe and stretch you at the end of the day.

rooms	10: 2 doubles, 2 singles, 6 suites.
price	€124–€276. Singles €73–€103. Suites €144–€276.
meals	Restaurants 2-minute walk.
closed	May-June; October-November.
directions	Exit S16 at St Anton & follow signs to tourist office. Hotel next to Galzigbahn cable car.

Hotel

piste or lift	10m	
cross-country trail	150m	tel +43 (0)5446 2220
lift for bikes	20m	fax +43 (0)5446 2253
village centre	100m	e-mail info@bergschloessl.at
		web www.bergschloessl.at

Johanna Moosbrugger

Map 2 Entry 5

Himmlhof
Im Gries 9, 6580 St Anton, Arlberg, Austria

Immaculately Tyrolean, the two-year-old chalet hotel trumpets every modern luxury. Its hub is its sitting room, warm with angelic frescoes on ceilings and walls, oriental rugs and open fire. Comfy Austrian sofas and easy chairs mix with the wrought-ironwork of candlesticks and curtain rails; the feel is traditionally alpine, yet all is new. Breakfast sets you up for the day, served in a half-panelled stübe on red gingham tablecloths. Upstairs, the scent of new pinewood fills cosy bedrooms heated by traditional tiled stoves. Floors are warmly wooden, there are sofas in the bigger rooms, a neat stack of logs for the fire, perhaps an antique carving of the Virgin Mary. The suites are gorgeous, their ornately carved, light-larch four-posters piled high with white duvets and pillows. Beneath the chalet the family have added a vaulted wellness area; the Italian checked floor and the cherubs may not be to everyone's taste but the steam room, sauna and thermal pool surely will be. The 'capital of the Arlberg', entertaining by day and night, is outside the door.

rooms	16: 12 twins/doubles, 4 suites for 2-4.
price	€ 110–€ 204. Suites € 148–€ 456.
meals	Restaurants nearby.
closed	May-June; mid-September-mid-December.
directions	Exit S16 at St Anton; right just before train station on to Stocklweg, then 1st left. Hotel on left.

Hotel

	Penz Staffler		
tel	+43 (0)5446 2322	piste or lift	200m
fax	+43 (0)5446 2322	cross-country trail	200m
e-mail	himmlhof@st-anton.at	lift for bikes	200m
web	www.himmlhof.com	village centre	10m

Map 2 Entry 6

Goldener Adler
6561 Ischgl, Austria

One of the oldest buildings in buzzing, well-to-do Ischgl has a glinting golden eagle on its 350-year-old sign. Inside: Scandinavia meets zen – the fourth generation of Kurzs have transformed the gasthof into a temple of modern design. Immaculate pine in floor and beam, pale sofas, low tables, a stainless steel fireplace crackling with logs, a warm glow: both bar and living room are comfortable, snug even. Plain beds lie on smooth floors, clean lines are softened by white duvets, fresh walls emboldened by stunning mountain photography. Some rooms have a wardrobe area partitioned by glass tiles, others by paper screens. Bathrooms sparkle with mosaics, showers are big, tubs deep. Each room is individual, each with a designer edge. Relax and unwind – or let the wellness centre do it for you. Spa, whirlpool, sauna, herbal bath; stone walls, frescos, uplighters, forest-green chairs. Food is freshly delicious, with a unique grain-free menu, and the skiing among the finest in Austria. In summer: trekking with llamas and prolific hiking – let your hostess be your guide.

rooms	30: 23 twins/doubles, 7 singles.
price	Half-board €79–€143 p.p.
meals	Half-board only.
closed	May-December.
directions	In centre of Ischgl.

Hotel

piste or lift	200m		Kurz Family
cross-country trail	1.5km	tel	+43 (0)5444 5217
lift for bikes	200m	fax	+43 (0)5444 5571
village centre	10m	e-mail	hotel@goldener-adler.at
		web	www.goldener-adler.at

Map 2 Entry 7

Haus Elisabeth
52, 6456 Obergurgl, Austria

A high altitude parish and a carvers' paradise, Obergurgl is relatively unknown to the British but has oodles of charm. And if you're looking for a cheerful place to stay where you can do your own thing, come here. The six modern apartments fit tidily inside a pretty white chalet, criss-crossed with wooden balconies, dotted with traditional windows. Inside, green painted pine sits on hexagonal, multi-toned tiles, walls are pine or plain, kitchens well-equipped. You have red and white gingham sofas, flowery curtains and the traditional ceramic green-tiled stove; framed prints decorate walls, there are wrought-iron lampstands, local pottery and baskets of dried flowers. The balconies face west and look to the glaciers of the 3,540m Schalfkogl that teems with black runs. In summer, the twisty drive to the end of the valley and over the pass into Italy is spectacular. And there's a garden to come back to. Sauna, ski room, washing machine and garage are shared, and the centre of the village is a step away.

rooms	6 apartments for 2-6.
price	For 2 €36–€90 per night; for 4 €84–€204; for 6 €126–€318.
meals	Self-catering. Restaurants 5-minute walk.
closed	Never.
directions	Road from Solden to Obergurgl; there, left after church; 150m; small road up hill; chalet 300m.

Self-catering

	Elisabeth Santer	piste or lift	300m
tel	+43 (0)5256 6257	cross-country trail	800m
fax	+43 (0)5256 62576	lift for bikes	1km
e-mail	elisabeth@obergurgl.com	village centre	300m
web	www.obergurgl.com/elisabeth		

Map 2 Entry 8

Jagdschloss Kühtai
6183 Kühtai, Austria

The great-grandson of Emperor Franz Joseph Karl Graf van Stolberg has turned the imperial hunting lodge into a winter sports hotel filled with character and tales to tell. His way is a personal one and he enjoys contact with guests; this makes the place special. Public rooms are white-walled or pine-clad... immaculate, subtly lit, aristocratic. Antique chests and Tyrolean chairs, copperplate engravings and hunting trophies from emperors and archdukes embellish every corner; no clutter, but a cosy feel. Bedrooms are divided between the lodge and the Elizabethian wing, with a further handful in the courtyard annexe. Some are modern and hotelly, others panelled in new pine; the best are the oldest and these are exceptional. In the intimate stübe feast on Austrian specialities such as fondue, raclette and seasonal game; wines come from a cellar that reaches deep into the mountainside. You're up high in Küthai so there are few trees but the scenery is stunning; the skiing is one of the Tyrol's best-kept secrets and you can schuss to the door. The village is a five-minute walk.

rooms	38: 35 twins/doubles, 2 suites, 1 apartment.
price	Half-board €115–€178 p.p.
meals	Half-board only.
closed	15 April–10 December.
directions	A12 Innsbruck & Breganz; exit Kematen, Sellraintal & Kühtai; hotel on right at end of village.

Hotel

piste or lift	500m
cross-country trail	500m
village centre	500m

Count Christian zu Stolberg-Stolberg

tel	+43 (0)5239 5201
fax	+43 (0)5239 5281
e-mail	info@jagdschloss.at
web	www.jagdschloss.at

Map 2 Entry 9

Gasthof Larchenwald
Lärchenwald 3, 6162 Mutters, Tirol, Austria

Mutters can't seem to stop winning the 'most beautiful village in Tyrol' prize.
This guesthouse sits on its meadowed fringe, a tall, early 20th-century chalet.
It's a warm family home run beautifully by Gretl and her two daughters, the old
panelled stübe at its heart. Chunky wooden benches dressed with dove-blue
cushions wrap around the traditional ceramic stove, tables are cosily Tyrolean.
Up the carpeted wooden stair are the bedrooms, four of which have their own
bathrooms and a small sitting area. They're all traditionally furnished, all different,
and some have a balcony. People travel some way for the food – country
traditional with a modern touch. Vegetables are seasonal and home-grown.
The skiing isn't bad either, in this area that has hosted two Olympic games. (And
an extended lift system is in the pipeline.) In summer there's a wooden terrace
lushly lined with geraniums – and some of the loveliest views in the world.
Innsbruck twinkles below as darkness falls.

rooms	10 doubles.
price	€ 48–€ 90.
meals	Lunch/dinner € 15.
closed	Rarely.
directions	From Innsbruck, Brennerstrasse, past ski jump, to Mutters. Gasthof signed.

Hotel

	Fam. Wishaber
tel	+43 (0)512 548 000
fax	+43 (0)512 548 000 54
e-mail	laerchenwald@aon.at
web	www.laerchenwald-mutters.at

piste or lift	5.5km
cross-country trail	5km
lift for bikes	5.5km
village centre	150m

Map 3 Entry 10

Hotel Weisses Kreuz
Herzog Friedrichstrasse 31, 6020 Innsbruck, Tirol, Austria

The 13-year-old Wolfgang Amadeus Mozart stayed here in 1769. Smack in the heart of the old town, the tall, 500-year-old hotel still keeps its winding, central staircase; once surrounded by open courtyard, it is now protected by new-fangled glass. The reception area, with huge, mottled-granite pillars, is most impressive, while the pine-clad stübe has barely changed since the late 18th century, and has the original built-in dining benches. In the main restaurant, airy and light thanks to large, wooden-arched windows, Austrian buffet breakfasts are served. The 'White Cross' may be a big hotel but it comes with a quirky and personal feel, and no two bedrooms are the same: some have high ceilings and a crisp, pale décor; others cósy and rustic. Outside, a big golden metal sign, first mounted in 1665, glints in the sun, while pedestrianised Friedrichstrasse teems with souvenir shops and Tyrolean cafés serving outrageously sumptuous cakes. Beyond, museums, galleries, shops and all you'd expect from a proper-sized town.

rooms	51: 28 twins/doubles, 12 triples, 7 quadruples, 4 singles.
price	€85–€110. Singles €57–€61.
meals	Restaurants nearby.
closed	Never.
directions	Hotel in pedestrian centre. Hotel car park off Innrainstrasse, 100m away.

Hotel

piste or lift	1km		Josef Ortner
cross-country trail	5km	tel	+43 (0)512 594 79 0
lift for bikes	1km	fax	+43 (0)512 594 79 90
village centre	10m	e-mail	hotel@weisseskreuz.at
		web	www.weisseskreuz.at

Map 3 Entry 11

Zur Linde
Hungerburg, 6020 Innsbruck, Tirol, Austria

A tiny pension in a tiny village – perched high above the valley, linked to
Innsbruck by a winding road. The views are sensational – and you'll love them
most on those days when a mist hovers over the valley below. The house sits by
mature trees on a tiny country road, an old wisteria shinning up its gabled roof.
There's a neatly clipped lawn with fruit trees at the back, delightful in summer,
and a cheerful 'coffee terrace' at the front. Children's drawings brighten the
windows of the kindergarten on the ground floor; the gasthof hides its entrance at
the back. Inside, sombre 100-year-old panelling is enlivened by colourful ceramic
stoves and Herr Patscheider's collection of rare old prints. The four bedrooms,
each with windows opening to a balcony, have modern pine beds and chairs, the
odd family heirloom, a cushioned bench, showers. Elsewhere, panelled ceilings
are warmed by cosy lamps and small chandeliers. Catch the funicular down to
Innsbruck, or the cable car up to the lifts (you can ski back to the door). An old-
fashioned, warm-hearted place, ideal for an active break at any time of year.

rooms	4: 3 doubles, 1 family.
price	€58–€145.
meals	Restaurant nearby.
closed	Rarely.
directions	From river's north bank, turn up Hottingergasse for 3km. Guesthouse on left, just before cable car. Look for Hungerburg sign.

Bed & Breakfast

	Fam. Patscheider
tel	+43 (0)512 292345
fax	+43 (0)512 292345
e-mail	hotel.zurlinde@tirol.com
web	http://members.tirol.com/zurlinde

piste or lift	150m
cross-country trail	6km
lift for bikes	150m
village centre	3km

Map 3   Entry 12

Wilder Mann
Romerstrasse 212, 6072 Lans bei Innsbruck, Tirol, Austria

An old Roman road once led 16th-century pilgrims to the chapel at Lans. Latter-day travellers come for one of the oldest buildings in the hamlet, the white-stuccoed, wood-weathered house that's been putting up mountaineers for years. And feeding them (well) from its cluster of pine-clad stübes. Meandering from the arched and painted front door to the old barn at the back, each one is as atmospheric as the last, with quarry tiles, Tyrolean pieces, gleaming glasses on fresh white cloths, maybe a big old stove, an ornate mirror, a cuckoo clock, a rustic chandelier. And forget wienerschnitzel and chips: the menu here is Austrian gourmet. Bedrooms lie quietly and swishly across the street in a new chalet built in the old style, its carved balcony bright with geraniums in summer. Inside, white walls and pale panelling, light pine furniture on smart coir, striped curtains, plump duvets; bathrooms are fabulous. Sink into a deep green sofa and gaze through modern French windows to snowy peaks beyond. Breakfasts are heartily continental, and as good as lunch and dinner.

rooms	14: 12 twins/doubles, 2 singles.
price	€ 130–€ 144. Singles € 55–€ 62.
meals	À la carte restaurants.
closed	Never.
directions	A12 Salzburg-Munich, exit Halls; approx. 4km to Ambass/Aldrans; 2km to Lans; right at restaurant Isser Wert; inn on left.

Hotel

piste or lift	1.5km	
cross-country trail	1.5km	
lift for bikes	1.5km	
village centre	10m	

		Schatz Family
tel		+43 (0)512 377387
fax		+43 (0)512 379139
e-mail		info@wildermann-lans.at
web		www.wildermann-lans.at

Map 3 Entry 13

Gästehaus Larch
6236 Alpbach 737, Austria

Maria and Franz own Gasthaus Jakober – Alpbach's most heart-warming inn. Now they have a brand-new Special Place: a big, beautifully set-up chalet, a fusion of self-catering apartments and B&B. The whole place is a paean to light larch, with a clean, fresh, Scandinavian feel inside and out. Décor is simple modern: polished floors, pine furniture, bright sofas, red and white gingham, perhaps a painted Tyrolean chest. White plastered walls and big windows give an airy feel; bedrooms smell sweetly of new pine; all have balconies with fantastic views. The apartments have an open-plan dining, kitchen and sitting room area with a tiled floor; bedrooms, some with bunks, are tucked under the eaves; bathrooms with double sinks sparkle whitely. You have everything you need, from fluffy white towels to web access; Alpbach, one of the Alps' prettiest resorts, is a trot down the road. Fondue, schnapps, hot chocolate, glühwein are part of Alpbach's wintery charm – best sampled in the enticing, 400-year-old stübe of the Jakober. The village has long been a favourite of British families.

rooms	4 + 4: 4 doubles. 2 apartments for 2-4; 2 for 4-6.
price	€ 44–€ 80. Apartments € 50–€ 80 for 2.
meals	Breakfast € 5. Restaurants 10-minute walk.
closed	Never.
directions	Exit E60 at junction 32 to Brixlegg; left to Alpbach. Guesthouse on village outskirts.

Bed & Breakfast/Self-catering

	Maria & Franz Larch
tel	+43 (0)5336 5875
fax	+43 (0)5336 5351 20
e-mail	info@gaestehaus-larch.at
web	www.gaestehaus-larch.at

piste or lift	600m
cross-country trail	1km
lift for bikes	1km
village centre	600m

Map 3   Entry 14

Villa Mellon
Franz Walde Weg 1, 6370 Kitzbühel, Austria

A secluded leafy road brings you up to the back of the house; its fresh white walls and perfectly painted window surrounds tempt you inside. Named after the US banking family who once owned it – it was their summer pad – Villa Mellon is the grandest of pensions. The hall is sumptuous with old paintings and Louis XVI-style chairs, while the deep-red drawing room has the feel of a Scottish hunting lodge – rafters, leather-bound books, a stag's head above the log fire. The dining room by contrast is bright and airy: lemon walls, fresh lilies by a white piano. Sophisticated 'international' food is served at a long table on fine china; doors glide open in summer to a lovely garden, terrace and circular pool. First-floor bedrooms are indisputably impressive – high ceilings, architraves, cornices, chandeliers – while those above are more intimate. All are extravagant, with painted or upholstered bedheads, floral fabrics and soft lights. Views are breathtaking, the walk down to Kitzbühel is short, and Herta makes every guest feel special.

rooms	15 twins/doubles.
price	€ 100–€ 160. Half-board option.
meals	Dinner € 17–€ 22. Restaurants in village.
closed	Never.
directions	From Kitzbühel for Lebenberg. Right immediately after Hotel Astron; 1st left; 50m on right.

Hotel

piste or lift	300m
cross-country trail	1.5km
lift for bikes	1km
village centre	600m

Herta Scheiterbauer
tel	+43 (0)5356 66821
fax	+43 (0)5356 66825
e-mail	info@villa-mellon.at
web	www.villa-mellon.at

Map 3 Entry 15

Schloss Rosenegg
Rosenegg 58, A-6391 Fieberbrunn, Austria

Its 14th-century towers, crammed with armour and dungeons, gaze over the rooftops of Fieberbrunn and across the valley. The old armoury is linked to the rest of the hotel by an underground passage lined with flickering candles; for *Lord of the Rings* fans, this is heaven. Bedrooms are reached via spiral stone staircases and have rustic wardrobes, checked carpeted floors, lovely chunky pine benches. Suites come with decorative headboards and sofas, corridors with chests, suits of armour, sashes and spears. John Eberhardt's parents bought the Schloss in 1942 and remodelled it into a guesthouse; it boomed during the war, being the chosen domicile of German officers; recently it's been eased into the 21st century. Breakfast buffets in the Blue Saloon are elaborate affairs, dinner is candlelit in a mahogany-panelled room, and the delicious spa flaunts a sauna and steam room, solarium, gym and indoor/outdoor pool. Come for golf in summer, snow in winter, landscaped gardens and gentle luxury. The Eberhardts make you feel at home yet treat you like kings.

rooms	144: 117 twins/doubles, 27 suites for 2-4 & 4-6.
price	Half-board € 67–€ 100 p.p. Suite half-board € 79.50–€ 107 p.p.
meals	Half-board only.
closed	November.
directions	From Salzburg, signs to Bad Reichenhall; B178 to St Johann; left under r'way to Fieberbrunn; in Rosenegg centre, 1st part of Fieberbrunn.
Hotel	

	Eberhardt Family
tel	+43 (0)5354 56201
fax	+43 (0)5354 52378
e-mail	info@schlosshotel-rosenegg.com
web	www.schlosshotel-rosenegg.com

piste or lift	200m
cross-country trail	200m
lift for bikes	200m
village centre	10m

Map 3 Entry 16

Postman's Knock
Poststrasse 107, 118118 Pöstchen, Austria

A long cold winter of discontent. This chocolate-box chalet built of matches has low ceilings suitable for no one at all. Wooden floors, leaky roof, immovable shutters and a fake balcony are just some of the reasons why you might not want to stay. However, being stuck on a pole does have its advantages: you are safe from angry rottweilers, marauding bears and avalanches. Inside, the chips look excellent on the glossy menu; this arrives each morning, through the flap: I know of nowhere offering such variety (sad that it all tastes of cardboard). There is an impressive range of magazines and other reading matter; just mind you don't get snowed in by junk mail. In winter you may have to dig your way out so why not bring a shovel? Or build an igloo on the roof instead. With no heating it's hardly stuffy at minus 20 degrees, and there's a good draught; in summer, at 30°C, you're uncommonly warm. No other chalet in the entire Alps boasts such a temperature range. *Note closed days.*

rooms	1 box room.
price	€ 2 first-class; € 1 second.
meals	Tasteless.
closed	Weekends; bank holidays; school holidays; impromptu holidays; August.
directions	Left at the boulangerie & ask the postman.

Bed & Breakfast

piste or lift	50m	
cross-country trail	50m	
lift for bikes	600m	
village centre	600m	

		Herr Briefträger
tel		post only
fax		post only
e-mail		post@mailbox.slot
web		www.never-comfortable.com

Gasthaus Burg Heimfels
Heinfels 5, 9920 Heinfels, Tirol, Austria

This is something different: a restaurant with self-contained flats. They're warmly cosy, too. The 300-year-old mountain gatehouse squats below the ruins of a fortified castle, high up above Lienz. A restaurant with rooms until the 1970s, Burg Heimfels was reopened in 2002 by friendly Manuela; now it's a freshly whitewashed Tyrolean house with decorative inscriptions across the wall and beautifully painted window frames. Inside are atmosphere and history in spades. Oriental carpets grace old tiled floors; the dining table in the vaulted cellar is illuminated by candles in wrought-iron chandeliers. Bedrooms, comfortably homely, have nice old pine furniture and brand-new beds. You get kitchenettes in all, sitting rooms in most, tiled stoves in two (logs on the house) and a balcony in one. Toys, an outside play area, a library, a washing service and sensible pricing complete the family-friendly picture. The front rooms look onto fields and little Heinfels with its smattering of shops. Choose from tennis and white-water rafting, hiking and mountain biking – and every winter sport under the sun.

rooms	6: 2 doubles, 4 family rooms for 4.
price	€ 33–€ 49. Family rooms € 54–€ 76.
meals	Dinner € 14.
closed	November.
directions	From Lienz towards Pustertal; 30km to Heinfels; B&B on right.

Self-catering

	Familie Schneider	piste or lift		30m
tel	+43 (0)4842 20094	cross-country trail		30m
fax	+43 (0)4842 20094 30	lift for bikes		30m
e-mail	info@gasthaus-burgheimfels.com	village centre		200m
web	www.gasthaus-burgheimfels.com			

Map 3 Entry 18

Schlosswirt
Döllach 100, Kärnten, 9843 Grosskirchheim, Austria

You are immersed in nature – the old chalet sits in the Mölltal valley surrounded by national park. Come for Martina and her stable of Halflingers – these small gentle horses are yours to borrow. Inside the red-shuttered house, old white walls are decorated with grand portraits and mountain prints. A light varnished floor sweeps across the hall, warmed by colourful kilims, there are exposed beams and arched doors, fine antique chests, carved wooden chairs, wrought-iron candlesticks. Martina adds homely touches: a bowl of sweet apples, a vase of fresh flowers, a sprig of berries. Bedrooms are simple but cheerful, all different, some with a little piece of the carved balcony that winds its way around the house. Lace curtains frame windows, plump white duvets sit on dark beds; there's a steam room and sauna. The antler-ed stübe, with its pink tablecloths and hay-filled cushions, draws in the locals for five o'clock beer and wienerschnitzel before a roaring fire. Anton knows all there is to know about skiing, mountaineering and sleigh rides – make the most of these mesmerising surroundings.

rooms	22: 13 doubles, 2 singles, 2 family rooms, 5 suites.
price	€37–€77. Half-board €45–€85 p.p.
meals	Lunch and dinner available.
closed	Mid-April–mid May; mid-October–mid-December.
directions	From Lienz, signs to Spittal; at Dolsach, left to Winklern; Grosskirchheim 12km. Inn in village, set back, on right.
Hotel	

piste or lift	10m		Anton Sauper & Martina Unterwelz
cross-country trail	10m	tel	+43 (0)4825 411
lift for bikes	10m	fax	+43 (0)4825 411 165
village centre	50m	e-mail	schlosswirt@eunet.at
		web	www.alpinreiten.com

Map 4 Entry 19

Grüner Baum
Kötschachtal 25, 5640 Bad Gastein, Austria

There's a faded grandeur to Bad Gastein, its 1920s hotels clinging to the side of its narrow gorge. The 'Green Tree', built as a hunting lodge in 1831 and a short drive uphill, is an entire *hoteldorf* – a cluster of big and small gasthofs, chapel and barn. In the family since 1913, surrounded by garden and forest, this unaffected old place has long attracted a celebrity crowd. The feel in the stübe of the main house is darkly alpine, with its aged wood, green baroque-tiled stove, embroidered tablecloths and mounted antlers. Bedrooms, suites and 'apartments' (ideal for families, with their own living room and two bedrooms) vary from hotelly to characterful; all are steeped in comfort. Some are panelled but most are pastel-walled; there are floral or lace curtains, modern furniture, the odd antique bed or lovely Austrian painted door, wooden sleigh or stained-glass window (depicting a hunting scene – what else!). With its library, conservatory, several bars, children's club and spa, this would be a marvellous place for a family get-together. Skiing is a shuttle away, horse-drawn sleighs wait by the door.

rooms	80: 35 twins/doubles, 25 singles, 20 suites for 2-4.
price	€160–€310.
meals	Dinner €25–€75.
closed	Never.
directions	From Salzburg, A10 for Villach, exit Bischofshofen on B167 to Lend; left for Gasteinertal. In Bad Gastein, right, up hill, past train station. Left after supermarket for 300m; left again for 3km.
Hotel	

	Johanna Blumschein	
tel	+43 (0)6434 2516 0	
fax	+43 (0)6434 2516 25	
e-mail	info@grunerbaum.com	
web	www.grunerbaum.com	

piste or lift	4km
cross-country trail	30m
lift for bikes	4km
village centre	4km

Map 4 Entry 20

Active by Leitners
Sportplatzstrasse 755, 5710 Kaprun, BZ, Austria

Action packages, ski safari, biking, fitness, tennis – the name says it all. This is a concept hotel with a 1960s feel: orange and yellow sofas are designer-square, curtains striped, small alcoves are built into white walls. Large wood-and-glass doors swing to a sunny breakfast room for buffet spreads of ham, eggs, local yogurt and homemade muesli; for all-day snacks – and after-ski cake, coffee, tea or something stronger – head for the bar. Upstairs you have a mix of sizeable apartments with kitchenettes – ideal for families – and 'feel-good' rooms; in spite of fairly standard fabrics and furniture, each has a warm feel and a balcony view. The number of sports on offer, especially in summer, is splendid: cycling and hiking trails start from the door, and you're a two-minute walk to the ski bus that gets you to the slopes. (Or the village, for hot chocolate and shopping.) Rosmarie and Wolfgang organise summer sports for kids, have special areas for sledging and snowball-throwing, and a 'partner' restaurant with its own children's corner close by. *Ask about ski, cycle and other holiday package deals.*

rooms	21 + 7: 21 twins/doubles. 7 apartments for 2-4.
price	€78-€128. Apartments €66-€196.
meals	Snacks available; half-board option at restaurants nearby.
closed	Rarely.
directions	From Zell am See, signs to Kaprun. On round village; 1st left after volleyball court into Sportplatzstrasse; 2nd road on right.
Hotel	

piste or lift	1.5km		Rosmarie & Wolfgang Leitner
cross-country trail	1km	tel	+43 (0)6547 8782
lift for bikes	1.5km	fax	+43 (0)6547 8782 59
village centre	250m	e-mail	info@active-kaprun.at
		web	www.active-kaprun.at

Map 4 Entry 21

Villa Klothilde
Skiliftstrasse 2-4, 5700 Zell am See, Austria

The old country house has been joined by a new chalet, bursting with apartments
and rooms and linked by a lift. Both sit in a manicured garden, set back from the
quiet road that leads to the town centre. Bedrooms are not homely but superbly
finished, with perfect white walls, simple pine furniture, built-in wardrobes, full-
length mirrors and modern, appealing fabrics. The most characterful sit under the
eaves. Three generations run the Klothilde, named after Grandma herself, with
energetic Daniela the youngest in line. She loves welcoming English-speaking
guests and has poured heart and soul into the recent renovations. Breakfasts are
buffet-style and generous. Zell am See wraps its smart self around two sides of
one of Austria's loveliest lakes, which freezes in winter; the medieval, car-free
centre teems with tea shops, restaurants, bars, clubs and boutiques. It's all
walkable, and the ski lifts are close. Watersports, not surprisingly, are the big pull
in summer.

rooms	17 + 5: 15 twins/doubles, 2 suites. 5 apartments for 2-6.
price	€ 52–€ 96. Apartments € 65–€ 170.
meals	Restaurants nearby.
closed	Rarely.
directions	From Saalfelden into Zell am See, after second traffic lights, up on right.

Bed & Breakfast

	Daniela Haslinger	piste or lift	200m
tel	+43 (0)6542 72660	cross-country trail	200m
fax	+43 (0)6542 72660	lift for bikes	200m
e-mail	info@pension-klothilde.at	village centre	500m
web	www.villa-klothilde.at		

Map 4   Entry 22

Photography by Nick Woodford

france

La Ferme de Nant
La Ville du Nant, 74360 La Chapelle d'Abondance, Haute-Savoie, France

Upstairs is chic and contemporary, downstairs traditional. Susie and Steve have transformed the 1789 farmhouse into a superb chalet that's fully catered in winter; floor-to-ceiling windows opening to a sunny balcony pull in the views. The open-plan kitchen/living/dining area is vast, with doors off to the bedrooms, floors are wooden and gleaming, halogen spots illuminate white walls, there's a mix of Savoyard and modern and a giant pop art portrait to add a sparkle. From the first floor you descend the stairs – past a fascinating collection of old wooden sledges that came with the house – to the more traditionally furnished ground floor. This is a delightfully cosy space with an open fireplace in the middle, good new sofas and beautiful country-antique dining room table and chairs. A trap-door leads to a cellar packed with DVDs, yours for winter evenings; the slopey garden has been reshaped to make way for a good-sized, heated pool, open from March. In winter the owners, who live on the top floor with their labrador, can drive you to the pistes. Susie also owns a horse and the riding is wonderful.

rooms	6 doubles/twins. Extra beds.
price	B&B € 100. Self-catering per week: 1 floor € 1,200; 2 floors € 2,250. Winter: € 785–€ 1,125 p.p. p.w.
meals	Dinner € 22. Self-catering June-August. Catered in winter.
closed	May & October-November.
directions	D22 for Chatel; through La Chapelle; left at sign for La Croix. On 3nd bend.

Self-catering/Catered/B&B

piste or lift	1km	
cross-country trail	1.5km	
lift for bikes	2km	
village centre	1.5km	

	Susie Ward
tel	+44 (0)1872 553055
fax	+44 (0)450 734087
e-mail	susie@susieward.com
web	www.susieward.com

Map 5   Entry 23

Chalet Gueret
La Villaz, 74110 Essert Romand, Haute-Savoie, France

You're spoiled rotten: a hot tub in the garden, a sauna, a games room, a heated swimming pool in summer, a library, an office with internet, a minibus to take you to the slopes. The chalet, rebuilt on the site of an ancient farmhouse, is five-years-new, swishly wooded and custom-made. Your sitting/dining room is large, with red sofa-ed seating for up to 14, an antique walnut table, ladderback chairs, good lamps, music and an open fire. Doors open to a balcony with a view and every single room has one (that or a terrace). Behind you are fields, in front the hamlet, and the deep Montriond Valley stretches beyond. Bedrooms, spread over first and second floors, are gorgeous in their woody garb: dark hardwood boat beds, crisp white linen, cast-iron baths. Michael and Katie Rumbold have been skiing forever and their enthusiasm for the mountains will inspire you: charming Morzine (five minutes in their minibus), gentle Les Gets, futuristic Avoriaz, and the biggest skiable/snowboardable domain in the world. Katie knocks up four-course feasts at dinner and the cuisine is 'haute'.

rooms	6: 4 doubles, 2 twins/doubles. Extra beds available.
price	£450-£930 p.p. per week.
meals	Catered.
closed	May-June; September-November.
directions	A40, exit 18. D902 for Les Gets & Morzine; road swings left after Hotel de Savoie. Left at next junc., for E. Romand. Till church; left up hill; right at top; 2nd chalet on left.

Catered

	Michael & Katie Rumbold
tel	+ 44 (0)1884 256542
	+33 (0)4 50 74 87 76 (chalet)
e-mail	info@chaletgueret.com
web	www.chaletgueret.com

piste or lift	3km
cross-country trail	3km
lift for bikes	3km
village centre	3km

Map 5   Entry 24

Au Coin du Feu - Chilly Powder
BP 116, 74110 Morzine, Haute-Savoie, France

The homeward piste takes you to the door; the cable car, opposite, sweeps you to the peaks. The chalet is named after its magnificent central fireplace… on one side gleaming leather sofas, on the other, red dining chairs at a long table. Everything feels generous here: great beams span the chalet's length, windows look up to the cliffs of the Hauts Forts, high ceilings give a sense of space. There's a reading room on the mezzanine above the living area with books, internet, antique globe and worn leather armchairs, and a small bar made of English oak by a carpenter friend. Bedrooms are alpine-swish and themed: there's the Toy Room for families, the English Room that sports a bowler hat. The carpets are sisal, one room's four-poster is veiled in muslin and the bathrooms have soaps from New Zealand and shower heads as big as plates. The chef produces the best of country cooking, and Paul and Francesca can organise everything, including torchlight descents. There's massage, a sauna, a hot tub outdoors, DVDs to cheer wet days – even an in-house nanny.

rooms	17: 6 doubles, 3 twins, 1 triple, 7 family rooms for 2-5.
price	€60. Winter: €457-€845 p.p. per week.
meals	Picnic lunch €5. Dinner €30. Catered in winter.
closed	Never.
directions	From Morzine, signs to Avoriaz, then Les Prodains; 2.8km; on right, just before cable car.

Bed & Breakfast/Catered

piste or lift	50m		Paul & Francesca Eyre	
cross-country trail	1.5km	tel	+33 (0)4 50 74 75 21	
lift for bikes	100m	fax	+33 (0)4 50 79 01 48	
village centre	3.5km	e-mail	paul@chillypowder.com	
		web	www.chillypowder.com	

Map 5 Entry 25

Chalet-Hôtel Crychar
136 impasse de la Grange Neuve, 74260 Les Gets, Haute-Savoie, France

Walkers and skiers are in heaven. Three sides face fields, you're right on the piste and three steps from the village. This is a traditional-style chalet built in 1984; geraniums trail from balconies, there's a decked terrace (skiers drop by for Greg's Breton crêpes), an outdoor pool and a delicious sauna. Enter to the aroma of wood and a cosily alpine feel. In the restaurant are red and white checked curtains, yellow-clothed tables, a big log fire, traditional pine and the freshest local produce, chosen by Greg each morning. He's in charge of food, and wife Cécile and her mother Yvette are in charge of décor – every brightly patterned curtain and bedspread has been handmade. (The little tapestries and patchworks that are dotted around the hotel are also their handiwork.) Beds are new and comfortable, walls are wooden-clad, most rooms have a balcony and three have a little mezzanine for a child's bed. Les Gets is a farming community that has blossomed, with a scattering of shops, bars, a night club, and one of the few ski schools in France that uses only British instructors. Brilliant for active families.

rooms	15: 5 doubles, 4 twins, 3 triples, 3 quadruples.
price	Half-board €67-€125 p.p.
meals	Half-board only.
closed	Mid-April-end-June; mid-September-20 December.
directions	D902 Les Gets; there, right at 2nd r'bout, for village centre; 1st main right; left at T-junc. for 30m; right for chalet-hotel. At end of road, signed.
Hotel	

	Yvette Bouchet
tel	+33 (0)4 50 75 80 50
fax	+33 (0)4 50 79 83 12
e-mail	info@crychar.com
web	www.crychar.com

piste or lift	10m
cross-country trail	400m
lift for bikes	200m
village centre	400m

Map 5 Entry 26

Chalet Elise des Alpes

Route des Grandes Alpes, 74260 Les Gets, Haute-Savoie, France

Dinners, prepared by the chef, are four-course treats, teas come with scrummy cakes, breakfasts are hale and hearty, children's suppers thoughtfully presented; Stuart also owns a restaurant so you're royally looked after. This new chalet looks like it's been here for ever, its 'toasted' timbers bestowing instant character. And Nikki's clever, light touch is sensed the moment you enter. You get traditional-style Savoyard sofas lined with country cushions; gingham curtains hugging windows; sparkling white bowls in pine-clad bathrooms; colourful rugs on light oak floors. The sitting/dining room on the first floor makes the most of the exposed beams supporting the roof, the log-fuelled hearth glows at its centre. Old cow bells hang from one beam, electronic wizardry and books and games await in the corner. Be enchanted by the views from the big corner balcony; sink into the hot tub on the terrace below. There's a sauna too. Bedrooms are divided between the ground floor and those with west-facing balconies – all are deliciously cosy. Attractive Les Gets is a short stroll.

rooms	Chalet for 12: 2 doubles, 1 twin, 1 triple, 1 family.
price	€ 1,000–€ 1,500 per week. Winter: € 750–€ 1,250 p.p. per week.
meals	Self-catering. Catered in winter.
closed	Rarely.
directions	Bypass around Les Gets for Morzine. 200m after 2nd roundabout, chalet set back, on left.

Self-catering/Catered

piste or lift	300m		Stuart & Nikki Redcliffe
cross-country trail	1.5km	tel	+33 (0)3 85 44 83 95
lift for bikes	300m	fax	+33 (0)3 85 44 90 18
village centre	100m	e-mail	info@highsocietyski.com
		web	www.highsocietyski.com

Map 5   Entry 27

Ferme de Montagne
La Turche, 74260 Les Gets, Haute-Savoie, France

The renovated Savoyard farmhouse opened its doors in 2001 – expect sheer luxury, embellished with wonderful finds. A stone floor from Burgundy, a zinc-topped bar from Paris, a 1930s beech butcher's block, two ornate lanterns from an old bridge in Bordeaux. Every piece of furniture is special, in this living space dominated by a central open fire. Bedrooms, all en suite, come with big baths, swan-necked taps and heated, steam-free mirrors; three of the rooms can be combined to create a family suite. There's Australian wool on perfect mattresses, bathrobes and thick towels, Frette linen and slippers, toiletries from Jo Malone, Michelin-starred cooking and exceptional wines. Traditional windows look onto flower-filled meadows in summer, virgin piste in winter and the bubbling hot tub all year round. (You get sauna and spa treatments, too.) Perched above Les Gets, the Ferme is a snowball's throw from pistes and lifts, and the team includes friendly ski guides to ease you into the terrain (no extra charge!). The village is a 10-minute walk or two-minute chauffeured drive.

rooms	8: 3 doubles, 5 twins.
price	£950-£1,750 p.p. per week.
meals	Catered.
closed	May; October-November.
directions	D902 to Les Gets. At 1st r'bout, 1st exit for village centre; 1st right for 2.5km to La Turche. After ski lift on left, old mazot on right. Chalet behind, set back from road.

Catered

	Suzanne Dixon-Hudson
tel	+33 (0)4 50 75 36 79
fax	+33 (0)4 50 75 51 03
e-mail	enquiries@fermedemontagne.com
web	www.fermedemontagne.com

piste or lift	50m
cross-country trail	800m
lift for bikes	1.5km
village centre	1.5km

Map 5   Entry 28

Chalet-Hôtel La Marmotte
61 rue du Chêne, 74260 Les Gets, Haute-Savoie, France

At the foot of the slopes on the edge of the village, the 1930s chalet has grown. But, thanks to its owners (a brother and sister team), it has never lost its family feel. It's a woodily warm and attractive place to stay, the panelled ceiling in the living room being especially lovely. Watch the last skiers trudge home as you relax on a wooden Savoyard sofa softened by lemon-yellow cushions before a big fire. In the dining room: checked red and white curtains, a fresh feel and a regional menu served once a week; Josette's fondues are a speciality. Bedrooms are a good size with quilted, comfortable beds; some have a small sitting area and a mezzanine, some a balcony facing the pistes. Other luxuries include a pool and fitness room, hammam, hydromassage and sauna, even a winter crêche for children. In summer the area is a cyclist's delight, there are marked trails, a freshwater lake for swimming, an adventure playground nearby, and free entry to the local golf club. A music festival is held in Les Gets every other year. It couldn't be better for families.

rooms	48 twins/doubles.
price	€ 119–€ 258.
	Half-board € 70–€ 195 p.p.
meals	Dinner € 30.
	In winter, half-board only.
closed	20 April-28 June;
	7 September-20 December.
directions	A40 exit Cluses for Les Gets; 22km; left at Hotel Chinfrey, right at 1st r'bout for Centre Station; right at end of road. On left.
Hotel	

piste or lift	50m		Josette Mirigay
cross-country trail	700m	tel	+33 (0)4 50 75 80 33
lift for bikes	50m	fax	+33 (0)4 50 75 83 26
village centre	100m	e-mail	info@hotel-marmotte.com
		web	www.hotel-marmotte.com

Map 5 Entry 29

Chalet Bossetan
Les Nants, 74110 Morzine, Haute-Savoie, France

Right on the piste and a five-minute swoop into town along a green run – perfect for novices. So the position couldn't be better – though the climb back after the lifts have closed is best avoided! Designed by a local architect, the Bossetan has floor-to-ceiling windows that set it apart from the more traditional chalet. Inside is an inviting family home. On the ground floor, a bleached wood, open-plan living area and a separate studio bedroom; upstairs, three more bedrooms. The living/dining area is warm with kilims, matching sofas and a stone-clad wood-burning stove, while the well-equipped kitchen gleams with its green-granite work surface and stainless steel oven. Up solid wooden stairs to large, light, airy rooms with beautiful sloping beams. You have everything you need here, from ski room to satellite TV, and the views are spectacular, even from the bath. Gaze through those picture windows to the waterfalls of the Valle des Ardoisières in spring, the snow-capped peaks of the Dents Blanches in summer and the twinkling lights of the village at Christmas.

rooms	Chalet for 10: 2 doubles, 3 twins.
price	Chalet: £950–£2,400 per week.
meals	Self-catering. Restaurant 500m.
closed	Never.
directions	Exit Route des Grandes Alpes for Morzine. Along Avenue de la Joux Plane to r'bout Rond Point de Joux Plane; 3rd exit for Les Nants. Hair-pin bend, chalet 100m on right.

Self-catering

	Louis & Ros Woodford
tel	+44 (0)1225 329129
e-mail	ros@woodford80.freeserve.co.uk
web	www.chaletbossetan.co.uk

piste or lift	10m
cross-country trail	1.2km
lift for bikes	1.2km
village centre	1km

Map 5 Entry 30

The Farmhouse

Le Mas de la Coutettaz, 74110 Morzine, Haute-Savoie, France

Dorrien once had the job of hunting out chalets for a ski operator. Which lead him to this 1771 manoir. He fell in love with it, learnt it was for sale, took it on. By Christmas 1994 the delightful worn leather armchairs, kilim rugs, claw-foot baths and wrought-iron beds were in, and look as though they've been here for ever – in tune with the great slabs of slate floor, worn smooth from three centuries' use. There's much Savoyard furniture, too, and books and flowers. Dinners in the old cattle shed are candlelit and huge fun; in winter, log fires blaze. Outside is a beautiful garden with roses clambering up the wall, a natural spring feeding a carved stone trough and new rooms in the grange. Historically this is an important house – so much so that the Mairie made a desperate attempt to wrest it from Dorrien and turn it into a museum. The Mas is an excellent launch pad for the Avoriaz and Portes du Soleil ski area, and Dorrien provides a ski host to introduce you to the runs. Deeply authentic, very special – and the pretty market town of Morzine lies down the road.

rooms	8: 3 doubles, 1 single, 3 family, 1 suite.
price	€80–€220. Singles €45–€140.
meals	Breakfast €10. Dinner with wine & coffee, €30–€40.
closed	May; October-November.
directions	In Morzine, signs for Avoriaz. Left on Avenue de Joux Plan after Nicholas Sport; right on Chemin de la Coutettaz. On left, next to youth hostel.

Hotel

piste or lift	250m	
cross-country trail	250m	
lift for bikes	350m	
village centre	300m	
		Dorrien Ricardo
tel		+33 (0)4 50 79 08 26
fax		+33 (0)4 50 79 18 53
e-mail		info@thefarmhouse.co.uk
web		www.thefarmhouse.co.uk

Map 5   Entry 31

Le Moulin du Bathieu

Vercland, 74340 Samoëns, Haute-Savoie, France

Perched on a hill above tiny, beautiful Samoëns is this old mill. Built over 100 years ago to crush oil from walnuts, it was turned into a hotel in the late 1950s by Pontet senior; now George has taken over the reins. An orchard still surrounds the little chalet and the scent of blossom wafts onto the terrace – a springlike accompaniment to fresh juice and local jams. The Moulin is very much a family affair: Anne cooks – beautifully – and the daughters clean. George's love is wine: ask for his list; it's an illustrated encyclopedia. Anne also loves sewing and dotted among the rustic furniture are samples of antique stitchwork and her own designs. After a glass or two of George's best, weave your way up the creaky pine stairs to bed – there's nowhere cosier than these woody, double-glazed rooms. Two sit under the eaves, each with a sitting area, a balcony and a mezzanine for extra beds; quilts are patterned or checked to match the curtains. Sleep with the window open and let the brook lull you to sleep. Skiers and walkers are five minues from the cable car, and there's a free ski bus.

rooms	7: 3 doubles, 1 twin, 2 duplexes for 3-4, 1 suite for 2-4.
price	€55-€130.
meals	Breakfast €8-€11. Dinner €20-€35.
closed	June; 4 November-21 December.
directions	A40 exit 18, onto D4; right on D254 for Samoëns. Hotel 1km on left.

Hotel

	Charles Pontet
tel	+33 (0)4 50 34 48 07
fax	+33 (0)4 50 34 43 25
e-mail	moulin.du.bathieu@wanadoo.fr
web	www.bathieu.com

piste or lift	500m
cross-country trail	1km
lift for bikes	2km
village centre	2km

Map 5 Entry 32

Le Château du Bérouze
74340 Samoëns, Haute-Savoie, France

Probably the finest manor in Samoëns. It's very old – the main part dates back to 1485 – yet six years ago it was on the verge of being demolished. New Zealand journalists Jack and Jane came to the rescue, poured love and talent into reviving old timbers and stones, then opened the large and extravagantly carved doors to guests. Up the stone steps to an elegantly proportioned, first-floor apartment, perfectly restored. You get an ample, open-plan kitchen, a modern living room, and bedrooms sharing two bathrooms, one with a claw-foot bath. Lofty ceilings are a criss-cross of white beams, lintels are ancient stone, floors rug-strewn, fireplaces vast, and big old radiators keep you warm. Outside is a garden that is every bit as lovely, with lush lawns, orchard and flowers, terrace and potager. A moat surrounds the house; streams flow in and out, home to ducks and trout. It's a special place in every season: come for skiing and skating in winter, rafting and riding in summer, high hiking in spring. Shops and bars are a five-minute trot, and your kind hosts will babysit if you ask them.

rooms	House for 8: 2 twins/doubles, 1 quadruple.
price	£850–£1,500 per week.
meals	Self-catering.
closed	Never.
directions	D907 to Samoëns. After large 'Welcome to Samoëns' sign, old church on left, house opposite on right.

Self-catering

piste or lift	1km		Jack & Jane Tresidder	
cross-country trail	200m	tel	+33 (0)4 50 34 95 72	
lift for bikes	1km	fax	+33 (0)4 50 34 95 91	
village centre	500m	e-mail	jane.tresidder@libertysurf.fr	
		web	www.chateauduberouze.com	

Map 5 Entry 33

L'Abbaye
74340 Samoëns, Haute-Savoie, France

A carved wooden drinking trough still stands by the front door; at the back is the steep grassy mound that led to where the animals stood (now, your comfortable living quarters). The big old farmhouse high above beautiful Samoëns is surrounded by undulating fields and comes with two outbuildings, two mazots, a barbecue, a bread oven and a Virgin Mary. Recently revived by the owners, L'Abbaye is a warm holiday home, perfect for (several) families. New quarry tiles cover the ground floor, dark wooden beams criss-cross the ceiling. You have an open-plan kitchen/dining/sitting room, a small library and a big log fire in the centre. Furniture is simple country style, lamps are modern, and the huge sofa, strewn with russet throws, is inviting. Wooden stairs lead to a mezzanine with TV, one bathroom, two showers and three bedrooms; fresh white walls are lined with ski photographs, paper lampshades add a glow. These rooms share a balcony with views over the garden and to the peaks beyond. Then up more stairs to a dormitory in the eaves: a bolthole for kids.

rooms	Chalet for 18: 4 twins, 1 room for 10.
price	€ 1,200–€ 3,850 per week.
meals	Self-catering. Restaurant 4km.
closed	Never.
directions	From Samoëns, left, for Col de la Joux Plane; 4km to chalet.

Self-catering

	Jean-Pierre & Martine Marchand	piste or lift	4km
tel	+33 (0)2 31 15 22 88	cross–country trail	4km
fax	+33 (0)2 31 15 22 89	lift for bikes	6km
e-mail	jpm-archi@mail.cpod.fr	village centre	4km

Map 5 Entry 34

Chalet Le Nanty

600 route du Pontet, La Frasse, 74300 Arâches, Haute-Savoie, France

A Portuguese stonemason built this chalet in 1943 as his dream home; now it is a simple and friendly guesthouse. Under the eaves are two white-walled rooms that share a balcony with mountain views. Colourful and simple textiles hang as bedheads with bedspreads to match; Helene changes the fabrics with the seasons. On the same floor is a living room area with a simple sofa, coffee table and books. Your hosts live on the floor below, give you good, simple breakfasts, and happily share their kitchen with large, stainless-steel oven (next to which stands a terracotta pot once used for salting an entire pig). Three nights a week Helene and Pierre cook for you – the food is delicious, and they use their own vegetables whenever possible. Down the stairs, atmospherically lit by an antique white lantern, are two more bedrooms and, sandwiched between them, is a large cosy living area with sofa. The bedrooms have floor-to-ceiling windows that open onto a small, decked terrace to the front, perched above a steeply-sloped garden. A free shuttle takes you from the hamlet of La Frasse to the lifts of Les Carroz.

rooms	2 suites (each with 2 twin/double rooms).
price	€60-€110.
meals	Dinner with wine & coffee, €20: Monday/Wednesday/Friday; otherwise self-catering.
closed	15 September-15 December.
directions	N205 from Cluses; D6 for Flaine & Les Carroz; 6.5km; lft in Arâches for La Fr.; 1st left. On left after 1st bend.

Bed & Breakfast/Self-catering

piste or lift	4.5km
cross-country trail	4.5km
lift for bikes	4.5km
village centre	4.5km

	Helene Esnault
tel	+33 (0)4 50 90 32 76
e-mail	lenanty@free.fr
web	lenanty.free.fr

Map 5 Entry 35

Chalet Odysseus
210 route de Lachat, 74300 Les Carroz d'Arâches, Haute-Savoie, France

Chalet Odysseus has the lot: comfort (soft sofas, bright rugs, open fire), swishness (satellite TV, sauna, small gym), a French chef who waves his gourmet wand over the dining table once a week, and English hosts who spoil you rotten. Kate and Barry lived in the village for seven years, then built their own house. They have the ground floor of this beautifully solid, purpose-built, brand-new chalet, you live above, and it's the sort of place you'd be happy in whatever the weather. Cheerfully pretty bedrooms come with the requisite pine garb, beds are covered in quilts handmade by Kate, two rooms have balconies that catch the sun, and the tiniest comes with bunk beds for kids. The shower rooms and bathroom are airy and light. As for Les Carroz, most skiers pass it by on their way to high-rise Flaine – a shame, for the village has heaps of character and several fine places to eat. Your own 4x4 gets you to the lifts in minutes, tying you in with the whole of the Grand Massif. Dinners are four-course and there's a *grole* night to boot. Great for a family break, whatever the season.

rooms	5: 3 doubles, 2 twins.
price	€ 90.
	Catered: € 495-€ 600 p.p. per week.
meals	Dinner with wine, € 40. Or rent as catered chalet.
closed	May & June; November.
directions	After Cluses N205, left onto D106. 7km before Les Carroz, red & white shuttered chalet on left; next left, signed.

Bed & Breakfast/Catered

	Kate & Barry Joyce	
tel	+33 (0)4 50 90 66 00	
fax	+33 (0)4 50 90 66 01	
e-mail	chaletodysseus@wanadoo.fr	
web	www.chaletodysseuslachat.com	

piste or lift	2km
cross-country trail	9km
lift for bikes	2km
village centre	2km

Map 5 Entry 36

Hôtel Les Servages d'Armelle

841 route des Servages, 74300 Les Carroz d'Arâches, Haute-Savoie, France

Rustic stone walls and low wooden ceilings greet skiers as they trudge in to the restaurant at the bottom of the piste. And there's Armelle, busily helping serve regional specialities as they flow from the kitchen: fondues and raclettes, Reblochon cheeses, smoked hams, *poulet fermier* with crayfish, herb-infused pork. Bedrooms, some small, are divided between a pretty cluster of buildings: some above the restaurant, the rest in little chalets that were brought down from high pastures and reconstructed – brilliantly – by Patrick. New and old are deliciously combined in rooms redolent with the smell of pine and beeswax. Chunky old timbers mix with bendy halogen lights and smoked-glass bathrooms, and some rooms have a mezzanine with space to tuck in an extra child. Comfortable beds are dressed in Egyptian cotton and white duckdown; all have a wood-burning stove. Gondolas close by link low-altitude Les Carroz with some dazzling skiing in the Grand Massif.

rooms	5: 3 doubles, 1 triples, 1 quadruple.
price	€160-€250.
meals	Breakfast €15. Dinner from €15. Half-board: extra €36-€50 p.p.
closed	May & November.
directions	D6 Cluses-Araches into D106 to Carroz d'Araches. 1st left past tourist office. At end of road.

Hotel

piste or lift	10m	
cross-country trail	900m	tel
lift for bikes	150m	fax
village centre	900m	e-mail
		web

Armelle & Patrick Linglin
tel   +33 (0)4 50 90 01 62
fax   +33 (0)4 50 90 39 41
e-mail   servages@wanadoo.fr
web   www.lescarroz.com/servages

Map 5 Entry 37

La Fontaine
Le Couteray, 74660 Vallorcine, Haute-Savoie, France

The chalet was built in 1739, half-way up a long winding road, its backdrop Mont Blanc. The restoration has been a two-year undertaking for Belgians Anne and Patrick, who used to rent the little place in the holidays, and fell in love with its unspoiled charm. Patrick restores furniture in his spare time and works at the Mairie down in Chamonix; Anne looks after their young son and her guests. Pass the fine stone drinking trough and the neatly stacked piles of wood, then up the three stone steps to the front door. Be greeted by an expanse of the palest larch – in ceiling, floor and wall. A long table dominates the kitchen/dining room, fruits ripen by one of two stoves, French windows open to a decked terrace. Up the creaky stairs to big rooms fresh with stripped pale pine. Fat checked pillows lie on white duvets, jolly rugs soften the floors, little lamps give a glow, halogen ceiling lights add a sparkle, bathrooms have heated rails. Cheese comes from the farm, recipes from the village (a shortish walk), and Cara the dog comes with a wag. It couldn't be nicer.

rooms	3: 2 doubles, 1 quadruple.
price	€70-€120.
meals	Dinner with wine, €17.
closed	Never.
directions	N506 Chamonix-Argentière. In Vallorcine, 3km before Swiss border, 1st left. Chalet on right after 2nd hairpin bend.

Bed & Breakfast

	Anne & Patrick de Plaen-Meys
tel	+33 (0)4 50 54 64 19
fax	+33 (0)4 50 54 64 19
e-mail	adp@lafontaine-vallorcine.com
web	www.lafontaine-vallorcine.com

piste or lift	700m
cross-country trail	900m
lift for bikes	700m
village centre	900m

Map 5 Entry 38

Villa Terrier
Route des Pecles, 74400 Chamonix, Haute-Savoie, France

A grand old 1910 villa in the middle of big, bustling, beautiful Chamonix. Sporting a smart new stone roof with shiny copper pipes, it looks across to Mont Blanc and the vertiginous Chamonix 'needles'. Ceilings are high, old pine spans the floors, original cornicing beautifies the walls. The living room is charming with an elegant mirror above a carved stone fireplace, rose sofas to sink into, grand lamps to read by, delightful drapes to draw across big windows; the kitchen (you can choose to self-cater) is large. Up the wide wooden staircase to light, roomy bedrooms, one with a balcony, two with sloping ceilings and more magnificent views. Some have huge bathrooms and, athough fabulously new, a traditional French feel, with their claw-foot baths, big sinks and fat iron radiators. White towels and bathrobes continue the mood of unashamed luxury. You get music and the internet, an indoor play area for children, lifts to the slopes and four-course dinners with wine. And a sauna and pool. Chamonix is the killer-black-run capital of Europe – and as popular in summer.

rooms	House for 8: 2 doubles, 2 twins/doubles.
price	£1,400-£3,000 per week.
	Catered £565-£755 p.p. p.w.
	Winter: £2,400-£4,800 p.w.
	Catered £665-£1,200 p.p. p.w.
meals	Self-catering or catered.
closed	Rarely.
directions	N506 Chamonix. Left at 1st r'bout for Chamonix Sud, over next 2 r'bouts & bridge to lights; left on Route des Pecles; 300m on right.

Self-catering/Catered

piste or lift	900m		
cross-country trail	1.5km	tel	+44 (0)1276 24262
lift for bikes	900m	fax	+44 (0)1276 27282
village centre	350m	e-mail	sales@collineige.com
		web	www.collineige.com

Colleen Olianti

Map 5 Entry 39

Mazot Les Tines
245 chemin de la Tannerie, 74401 Chamonix, Haute-Savoie, France

Shaded by poplars rustling in the wind is this mini-chalet. As the name implies, it was a wood store once – Colleen's. She is the owner, runs her own ski company, and lives across the garden. All is light and bright and stylishly decorated, with country furniture and modern checks. Downstairs is open plan. The dining area has a roundly rustic table for four, there's a shower room (with bathrobes), a washing machine and a kitchen with pottery and pine. The living area is cosy and charming: colourful textiles and prints grace pine-clad walls, there's a perfect red sofa, a little wood-burning stove, a stereo. A mezzanine, reached by a ladder, has two single mattresses and is suitable for kids; a floor-to-ceiling window looks onto the garden, filling the space with light. Up the wooden spiral stair to the bedroom with balcony and magnificent mountain views. An outside stair leads down to the garden, where roses clamber up wooden walls, geraniums fill window boxes, creepers weave through a pile of stacked slates. You are on the edge of lovely Les Tines and a bus brings you to even lovelier Chamonix.

rooms	Chalet for 4: 1 double, 1 mezzanine for 2.
price	£400-£700 per week.
meals	Self-catering. Restaurant 1km.
closed	Never.
directions	From Chamonix for Argentière. Left onto small road after golf course, just before railway; 200m on left.

Self-catering

	Colleen & Jean-Marie Olianti	piste or lift	1.5km
tel	+44 (0)1276 24262	cross-country trail	500m
fax	+44 (0)1276 27282	lift for bikes	1.5km
e-mail	sales@collineige.com	village centre	1.5km
web	www.collineige.com		

Map 5 Entry 40

Les Mazots
210 Montée Croix des Moussoux, 74400 Chamonix, Haute-Savoie, France

It's a steep road to get here: views over the Mont Blanc ranges soar. The 1930s-built chalet, in a quiet corner of Chamonix, is still only on its second careful owner. Colleen has run the house as a B&B for 12 years; now you can self-cater as well. In winter it's (mostly) catered. Chefs serve four-course dinners with good house wines, there's a minibus for those without cars, and masses of help with organising ski hire and lessons. The lovely house has a faded elegance, with much of the furniture left by the original owners: worn leather armchairs, wonderful sepia photographs of acrobats on dark panelled walls, shelves on the stairs crammed with old tomes. Crisp blue-and-white checked sofas sit under new reading lamps, the large wooden fireplace is decorated with candlesticks, and French windows open to the sloping garden with fruit trees and two pretty mazots (used as extra bedrooms). Bedrooms in the main house are a good size, comfortably furnished and traditional; fat duvets on antique iron beds (with new mattresses!) guarantee sound sleep. The kitchen has stainless-steel worktops and a large oven.

rooms	8: 2 doubles, 2 twins/doubles, 2 twins, 2 singles.
price	€80-€180; Wint. €80-€250. Self-c £1,500-£3,000; Wint. £2,500-£5,000 p.w. Catered £525-£725; Wint. £630-£1,120 p.p.p.w.
meals	Picnic €10. Dinner with wine, €35.
closed	Never.
directions	E25 Chamonix; left at 1st r'bout for Cham. Sud; over 2 r'bouts to lights; left for Les Bossons; 1st right up hill; on right.

Self-catering/Catered/B&B

piste or lift	750m		Colleen Olianti
cross-country trail	1.5km	tel	+33 (0)4 50 55 83 08
lift for bikes	750m	fax	+33 (0)4 50 53 51 91
village centre	750m	e-mail	sales@collineige.com
		web	www.collineige.com

Map 5   Entry 41

Hameau Albert 1er
38 route du Bouchet, 74402 Chamonix, Haute-Savoie, France

Under the current Carrier – exuberant chef Pierre – the railway hotel has become as famous for the delectability of its cuisine as for the comfort of its rooms. It's been in the family since 1903, named after Albert of Belgium who liked it so much he couldn't stay away. Rooms in the original villa, lofty and ornately corniced, were renovated in 2004. All are very fine, with beds dressed in perfect linen. Chalet Soli is no less luxurious and comes with its own sauna. Even more exquisite are the rooms in La Ferme, a little enclave on the edge of manicured gardens. Come for rustic chic and the most gorgeous bathrooms in Chamonix: woody, white-tiled and whirlpooled. There's also a half-in, half-out swimming pool for all weathers, with underwater spots and decked terrace, and a spa. In the grand dining room you feast like kings on the best of Piedmontese (gnocci with truffles, stuffed rabbit with herbs, pancetta and parsley jus), or delve into neo-peasant delicacies in La Maison Carrier. Vegetables come from the potager; the cellar guards vintages from 1947. World-renowned Chamonix is at your feet.

rooms	Albert 1er: 20 doubles. La Ferme: 12 suites. Chalet Soli for 4-6.
price	Albert 1er: € 115–€ 490. La Ferme: € 229–€ 890. Chalet € 800–€ 1,400.
meals	The Albert: € 54. La Maison Carrier: from € 26.
closed	9 November-3 December.
directions	From N506 Chamonix bypass, over railway bridge; at r'bout 1st exit for Argentière. Hotel 1st right.

Hotel

	Natalie Bernos	piste or lift	200m
tel	+33 (0)4 50 53 05 09	cross-country trail	50m
fax	+33 (0)4 50 55 95 48	lift for bikes	200m
e-mail	infos@hameaualbert.fr	village centre	100m
web	www.hameaualbert.fr		

Map 5 Entry 42

La Ferme d'en Haut
152 route des Aillouds, 74310 Les Houches, Haute-Savoie, France

Bubbly Mijo has transformed the 1833 farmhouse into an exceptional place to stay. High above Les Houches, surrounded by nature yet near Chamonix, you have the best of all worlds – pistes, hiking trails, sublime views. The summer garden is shaded by fruit trees; winter logs crackle in the big central fire. The charming living/dining room is open plan; a sloping wooden ceiling meets a white wall decorated with framed posters, furniture is red-cushioned Savoyard, simple rugs soften the floor, French windows open to a west-facing balcony. Find a perch on the carpet-covered logs and watch the sun dip down over the Mont Blanc range; there's a telescope to help you. Aperitifs are followed by delicious regional and French dishes, served at the convivial *table d'hôtes*. Bedrooms – downstairs – have rustic panelled walls, white ceilings, carved doors, pretty homemade throws, colourful prints. Country chests and wardrobes come courtesy of Mijo's family – or from antique shops in luscious Megève. *Minimum stay three nights.*

rooms	4: 3 twins/doubles, 1 triple.
price	€64.
meals	Half-board with wine & coffee, €50 p.p.
closed	Rarely.
directions	11km past Sallanches, for Les Houches. Through village to roundabout; 3km up hill, on right.

Bed & Breakfast

piste or lift	100m		Mijo Turc
cross-country trail	700m	tel	+33 (0)4 50 54 74 87
lift for bikes	1.3km	fax	+33 (0)4 50 54 74 87
village centre	1.3km	e-mail	mijoturc@aol.com
		web	www.lafermedenhaut.fr

Map 5 Entry 43

La Maison du Vernay

164 route de la Mollaz, 74170 St Gervais le Bains, Haute-Savoie, France

Caroline has brought charm to this purpose-built chalet-hotel turned B&B.
She's opened up rooms and added downlighters and new checked chairs to create
a mood of warmth; well-thumbed books line the shelves, flowers scent the air.
A big, chunky stone fireplace stands in the centre of the living room; round the
corner is the long *table d'hôtes* at which guests tuck into Caroline's regional treats.
Bedrooms are colour-themed according to the flower after which they are named:
Crocus, simply dressed in whites and blues, Rhododendron in reds and yellows.
Every room comes with a west-facing balcony and a mountain view, a softly
quilted bed, new wood on floors and walls and plenty of built-in hanging space.
White bathrooms sparkle. The St Gervais bubble is 900 yards from the door and
takes you up to Megève and the vast Mont Blanc playground; in spring and
summer the hiking, too, is superb. You're couldn't be nearer St Gervais, lively
with restaurants, Olympic ice rink, thermal spa and summer fêtes.

rooms	5: 3 twins/doubles, 2 quadruples.
price	€ 60–€ 132.
meals	Dinner € 18.
closed	Mid–April–mid–May; mid–August–mid–December.
directions	Exit A40 for Saint Gervais for 8km. Through village, road forks. Keep left, then 1st left. B&B on right.

Bed & Breakfast

	Caroline Marchal	piste or lift	900m
tel	+33 (0)4 50 47 07 55	cross–country trail	900m
fax	+33 (0)4 50 47 07 55	lift for bikes	900m
e-mail	info@lamaisonduvernay.com	village centre	200m
web	www.lamaisonduvernay.com		

Map 5 Entry 44

Les Fermes de Marie
Chemin de Riante Colline, 74120 Megève, Haute-Savoie, France

The cluster of weathered chalets has been dismantled from high pastures and reinvented to create an enticing *village de calme*. Savoyard furniture – much of it rescued from local farmhouses – is mixed with fresh modern checks and old gingham: heavenly rustic chic. The main chalet, home to reception and one of two restaurants, is like a decorated barn, its hay rack filled with cheesemaking paraphernalia from former days. Nine chalets are interlinked by underground passages in winter, built so as not to disturb the snow, and the beauty spa is renowned – for its pool, hammam, sauna and natural treatments based on edelweiss, gentian and melissa. Don cashmere and jeans for roast meats in the rôtisserie, or potatoes cooked in hay with sevruga caviar (a signature dish); retire with coffee to a book-filled salon by the fire. Then to bed: the sophisticated Sibuets have created seductive rooms with four-posters or open fires. All have aged-pine walls, beautiful checks, mod cons decoratively hidden. Step outside to 'the 21st arrondissement of Paris': Megève bustles stylishly all year.

rooms	71: 25 twins/doubles, 37 triples, 2 family rooms for 5, 7 suites.
price	€ 190-€ 770. Suites € 542-€ 786.
meals	Breakfast € 17. Dinner € 45-€ 150.
closed	Mid-October-mid-December.
directions	N212 from Sallanches, through Megève to 2nd of two large roundabouts; 3rd exit for 50m; left. Reception at end of road, signed.

Hotel

piste or lift	800m	
cross-country trail	1.5km	tel
lift for bikes	800m	fax
village centre	300m	e-mail
		web

Jocelyne & Jean-Louis Sibuet
tel   +33 (0)4 50 93 03 10
fax   +33 (0)4 50 93 09 84
e-mail contact@fermesdemarie.com
web   www.fermesdemarie.com

Map 5   Entry 45

Le Mont Blanc

Place de l'Eglise, Rue Ambroise Martin, 74120 Megève, Haute-Savoie, France

Jean Cocteau came to the Mont Blanc – his drawings festoon much of the ground floor – as did other literary luminaries. The celebrity parties that took place in the Fifties are legendary… there's nowhere as atmospheric as Megève's oldest and most famous hotel. Pine is king – find it in panelled walls, coffered ceilings, carved cornices, bedheads and chairs… even the foyer is a joy: soft sofas and carved chests, good pictures, gentle lights. Owner and decorator Jocelyne Sibuet has chosen wallpapers and fabrics that blend subtly and enticingly with the pale wood, then added antiques, paintings and traditional-style Savoyard furniture. Bedrooms are magnificent in their warm garb. Perhaps your quilted, multi-pillowed bed shelters in a frill-decked alcove? Several do. The sitting room is den-like, the spa is gorgeous (the same delicious treatments are used as at the sister hotel, Les Fermes de Marie), and the hot chocolate in the *salon de thé* is to die for. Staff appear as contented as their guests and it's worth every euro it takes to stay here. Voluptuous Megève lies at your feet.

rooms	40: 29 twins/doubles, 11 suites.
price	€ 196–€ 396. Singles € 160–€ 295. Suites € 362–€ 638.
meals	Breakfast € 15. Restaurants in Megève.
closed	Mid-April–mid-June.
directions	Exit A40 for Sallanches; N212 for Albertville for 13km to Megève. Hotel in village centre, signed.

Hotel

	Jocelyne & Jean-Louis Sibuet
tel	+33 (0)4 50 21 20 02
fax	+33 (0)4 50 21 45 28
e-mail	contact@hotelmontblanc.com
web	www.hotelmontblanc.com

piste or lift	100m
cross-country trail	1km
lift for bikes	100m
village centre	10m

Map 5 Entry 46

La Sauge
Les Evettes, Flumet, Savoie, France

A magical pair of chalets in a fruit-tree-filled garden near the end of the piste. The smaller of the two looks like a doll's house; up the stair to the wooden veranda, then into a tiny, cosy kitchen. The separate dining room is most appealing with its antique table and dresser and country chairs, and a pair of old-fashioned wooden skis is pinned to the pine-clad walls of the living room – typical of this chalet's mix of fine antiques and rustic pieces. Watch young children on the steep, ladder-like stair – it leads to a narrow mezzanine that overlooks the sitting room (with open fire) and to a cosy bedroom under the eaves. Twenty yards down the garden is the second, larger chalet. Built in the 1970s as a holiday home, it has been recently done up in a simple, functional style, is well-equipped, and has colourful rugs, locally-made furniture and an open fire adding warmth and character. You couldn't be in a more peaceful spot – or closer to the slopes. Shops are a couple of miles away, at Flumet, so take the car.

rooms	1 chalet for 4 (1 double, 1 mezzanine); 1 for 6 (1 double, 1 twin, 1 mezzanine with double).
price	€450–€800 per week.
meals	Self-catering. Picnic lunch €8. Restaurants 3km.
closed	Rarely.
directions	N212 Albertville-Megève; 3km after Flumet, right, for ski lift. Down rough track, on far side of car park.

Self-catering

piste or lift	10m		Samantha Acres	
cross–country trail	20m	tel	+33 (0)2 41 53 04 96	
lift for bikes	10m	e-mail	lasauge@aol.com	
village centre	3km	web	www.lasauge.com	

Map 5 Entry 47

La Touvière
73590 Flumet, Savoie, France

Mountains march past Mont Blanc and over into Italy, cows graze in the foreground – La Touvière is perfect for exploring this paradise. Myriam, bubbly and easy, adores having guests with everyone joining in the lively, lighthearted family atmosphere. In their typical old unsmart farmhouse, the cosy family room is the hub of life. Marcel is part-time home-improver, part-time farmer (just a few cows now). One bedroom has a properly snowy valley view that reaches all the way to Mont Blanc, the other overlooks the owners' second chalet, let as a gîte; rooms are small but not cramped, simple but not basic, with showers not baths. There's a table outside at which you can savour both sundowner and view. Eat here – dinners are sociable affairs – or hot-foot it to the nearest restaurant: 10 minutes down the hill (20 up!). Alternatively, drive the short distance to Megève, stuffed with restaurants, many chic. It's a charming and traditional resort that attracts a few famous faces – considering how close you are, this is remarkable value.

rooms	2 doubles.
price	€40.
meals	Dinner with wine, €15; book ahead.
closed	Rarely.
directions	From Albertville, N212 for Megève for 21km. After Flumet, left at Panoramic Hotel & follow signs.

Bed & Breakfast

	Marcel & Myriam Marin-Cudraz	
tel	+33 (0)4 79 31 70 11	

piste or lift	3km
cross-country trail	4km
lift for bikes	6km
village centre	3km

Map 5 Entry 48

L'Ancolie
Lac des Dronières, 74350 Cruseilles, Haute-Savoie, France

It may not be steeped in history but it is exceptionally welcoming, thanks to Yves. In its kept garden with woods behind and a lake at its feet, L'Ancolie was custom-built 10 years ago to replace the family's old guesthouse. Their aim was simple, to combine modern comforts with the best of tradition. So you have wooden balconies and fitted carpets, log fires in stone fireplaces and an open kitchen through which you can watch rich Savoyard specialities being prepared. In summer, restaurant doors swing open onto a terrace and everyone dines by the gently lapping waters. Big bedrooms, some with balconies, have modern furniture; luxury bed linen adds a touch of class; bathrooms are bang up to date. You may fish on the lake, walk from the door or have a round of golf – there's a course nearby. Delightful Annecy and cosmopolitan Geneva are only a half-hour drive away, and the hotel is as popular with families as with business folk. Watch the lake with young children.

rooms	10 doubles.
price	€ 71–€ 103.
meals	Breakfast € 11.
	Lunch & dinner € 25–€ 43.
	Restaurant closed Mondays.
closed	2 weeks in February (French school holidays).
directions	From Annecy, N201 to Cruseilles. In village, D15. Hotel immediately after Institut Aéronautique.

Hotel

piste or lift	150m		
cross-country trail	3km	tel	+33 (0)4 50 44 28 98
lift for bikes	150m	fax	+33 (0)4 50 44 09 73
village centre	150m	e-mail	info@lancolie.com
		web	www.lancolie.com

Yves Lefebvre

Map 5 Entry 49

Hôtel Auberge Camelia
74570 Aviernoz, Haute-Savoie, France

Roger knows his local history, and has stories about the Resistance: the previous owner of this auberge had connections with the clandestines. The Camelia was thoroughly modernised some years ago – now there's a small, intimate restaurant in what was the old kitchen, and the roomy bedrooms are smartly comfortable. Expect pretty new pine beds, armchairs, carpets and big bathrooms, and cattle strolling past the window, their alpine bells jangling. The delicious open garden has a spring-fed fountain and a sunny terrace where meals are served in fine weather in view of impressive hills. Suzanne and Roger have apparently boundless energy and will transport you in their red minibus to the start of some glorious walks – or to the lifts, a 45-minute drive. See the spectacular flower meadows, taste the wines, ski at all levels. A very welcoming inn with delightful owners and staff and a hotel dog who is so popular he gets his own web page. Food is Savoyard and good, and there's the occasional English theme night.

rooms	12: 5 doubles, 6 triples, 1 quadruple.	
price	€68–€98.	
meals	Breakfast €9. Lunch/dinner from €15.	
closed	Never.	
directions	N203 Annecy-Chamonix & La Roche; right at mini r'bout at Pont de Brogny, under r'way; 4km; right for Villaz on D175. There, keep left; left for Aviernoz. On left.	
Hotel		

	Suzanne & Roger Farrell-Cook	
tel	+33 (0)4 50 22 44 24	
fax	+33 (0)4 50 22 43 25	
e-mail	info@hotelcamelia.com	
web	www.hotelcamelia.com	

piste or lift	27km
cross-country trail	17km
lift for bikes	50m
village centre	27km

Map 5 Entry 50

La Bournerie
Le Chinaillon, 74450 Le Grand Bornand, Haute-Savoie, France

You arrive via 142 steps – not for the faint-hearted! But your reward is a
gloriously weathered, 200-year-old farmhouse-chalet that glows all year round.
On its ground floor is a small restaurant – pop in for a snifter of *grole*, the local
rum drink popular with skiers – and two breakfast rooms, one big, one small.
It's shoes off up the staircase (house rule) which, steep and ladder-like, takes you
up what was once the wooden chimney. Then into a living area under the eaves,
crammed with sofas, rugs, old-fashioned lamps and a small wood-burning stove.
Bedrooms fan off here and vary in size, from a small bunkroom to a big family
room with a child's room under the rafters. The restaurant specialises in simple,
diet-defying fondues and raclettes, perfect after a day spent hurtling down slopes.
In spite of its remoteness this is a wonderful place for families to stay, with a
friendly young owner who provides toys and books to keep everyone happy. Bags
are transported in winter via the ski lift that stops by the house; the slopes are a
scrunch away.

rooms	5: 2 doubles, 1 twin, 1 family room for 5, 1 bunk room for 4.
price	€34-€44 p.p.
meals	Half-board only.
closed	Never.
directions	From Annecy, D909 to St Jean de Sixt; D4 Grand Bornand & Chinaillon; 2nd right to slopes for 100m; steel steps up hill on right.

Bed & Breakfast

piste or lift	10m		
cross-country trail	800m	tel	+33 (0)4 50 27 00 28
lift for bikes	800m	fax	+33 (0)4 50 27 00 28
village centre	200m	web	www.legrandbornand.com

Sylvie Vadon

Map 5   Entry 51

Chalet Maxim
La Clusaz, Haute-Savoie, France

No wonder Steve and Janelle fell in love with La Clusaz – that Savoyard charm is irresistible. And this 'boutique chalet', newly fashioned from old wood from a nearby farm, feels as old as the hills. It's luxurious rusticity at its best: floors are terracotta, walls pine, and the four levels are dotted charmingly with old chests and wardrobes, kilims, fresh fabrics and pictures. The living room has a high-raftered ceiling and a mezzanine that looks down to the cosy, log-fired room below, stacked with games, DVDs and every modern comfort – these are experienced chalet hosts. Five bedrooms share four bathrooms (three en suite), and children get bunkbeds and their own meals, served early if you wish. Babysitters and creche are on tap too. In winter it's a fast schuss – or two-minute shuttle, courtesy of your hosts – to the lifts of the third oldest ski resort in France. In summer there's a garden with space for children and deckchairs for you. It's a short walk to La Clusaz; with its stylish shops and weekly market, ice rink, restaurants, bars and disco, it's one of the nicest family in the Massif.

rooms	Chalet for 12: 2 doubles, 1 twin, 1 family room, 1 children's room.
price	€ 850–€ 1,500 per week. Winter: € 580-£890 p.p. per week.
meals	Self-catering. Catered in winter.
closed	Rarely.
directions	Annecy for Les Aravis; at Thones r'bout for La Clusaz; there, 1st r'bout, 3rd left; next r'bout, left; pass chapel; 4th chalet on right, before bridge.

Self-catering/Catered

	Steve & Janelle Elsdon	piste or lift	50m
tel	+33 (0)4 50 63 10 95	cross-country trail	50m
e-mail	chaletmaxim1@tiscali.fr	lift for bikes	500m
web	www.chaletmaxim.com	village centre	500m

Map 5 Entry 52

Hôtel Le Calgary
73620 Les Saises, Savoie, France

From the outside it looks like two old gasthofs linked in the middle – yet, amazingly, it's new. Le Calgary was built by Les Saises's most famous son, Franck Picard, and named after the resort in which he gained his Olympic gold medal. Panelled ceilings span the open-plan sitting area and bar, dark antique furniture sits alongside modern coffee tables, there are big lamps, fresh flowers and an open fire. Patterned red rugs are strewn across the hardwearing green carpeting throughout the ground floor. Upstairs bedrooms have interesting carved doors, each with an original hand-painted design, and you have lots of light and space. The furniture is simple pine, and there are built-in cupboards and big windows with balconies and mountain views. If you want character, choose a room under the eaves. Jeannette and Jean-Jacques love having children to stay and give families a crèche, an indoor pool and supervised hours in the billiard room. And you're brilliantly positioned for shops and piste.

rooms	35: 6 doubles, 13 twins, 8 triples, 5 quadruples, 3 family rooms for 5.
price	€75. Winter: half-board only, €91–€129 p.p.
meals	Picnic lunch €8. Dinner €23.
closed	End-April-mid June; September-mid-December.
directions	From Albertville, D925 to La Pierre; left on D218b for Les Saises. On right at end of village.
Hotel	

piste or lift	150m	
cross-country trail	300m	tel +33 (0)4 79 38 98 38
lift for bikes	400m	fax +33 (0)4 79 38 98 00
village centre	10m	e-mail info@hotelcalgary.com
		web www.hotelcalgary.com

Fam. Berthod

Map 5 Entry 53

Chalet Kiana

1073 route de la Frasse, 74170 Les Contamines-Montjoie, Haute-Savoie, France

Jennie and David moved here four years ago and are great hosts. A welcome aperitif and canapés, help with ski hire and ski school, early supper for children – they do it all. (Note the winter price includes Saturday transfers and a ski guide on the first morning.) They built their chalet in the traditional way and plonked it in the perfect place: a lovely quiet spot on the edge of this pretty village. You have light and airy bedrooms named after glaciers, blond-pine walls and ceilings, balconies with splendid views. There are old pine cupboards, check curtains, comfy sofas round a log fire, books, games, video and DVD, and candlelit meals at a magnificent oak table. David's Landrover gets you to the lifts within minutes – though a shuttle also runs between the village and the gondolas. The skiing is superb, possibly the best in the world: un-crowded pistes, good snow... you could be swooshing down Chamonix's famous slopes within 25 minutes. Return to sauna and jacuzzi. Plenty of action in summer too, from tennis to rock climbing and donkey rides to great walks.

rooms	6 twins/doubles.	
price	€ 70-€ 90. Winter: € 720-€ 1,110 p.p. per week.	
meals	Dinner € 25; book ahead. Catered in winter.	
closed	May & October, November.	
directions	St Gervais D902 for Les C. In centre, 1st left after green pharmacy sign. After 1km & 5 bends, 2nd track on left. Sign under letter box.	

Bed & Breakfast/Catered

	Jennie & David Henderson	piste or lift	1km
tel	+33 (0)4 50 91 55 18	cross-country trail	2km
fax	+33 (0)4 50 91 55 38	lift for bikes	2km
e-mail	chaletkiana@aol.com	village centre	500m
web	www.chaletkiana.com		

Map 5 Entry 54

Chalet Les Carlines
Pré Berard, 73210 La Côte d'Aime, Savoie, France

Below the slopes of La Plagne and beyond the Vanoise National Park lies the tiny linear village of La Côte d'Aime – super-sunny but snow-light. If you do want to ski, snowboard or bobsleigh, the high-altitude ski arena of La Plagne and Les Arcs is a 15-minute drive. The house is new, designed in the local style. The cosy living room has an Alsatian feel with white crépy walls, carved wood, china plates and bottled genepi on display – small children are not encouraged! – and the atmosphere is homely. Carpeted bedrooms are large and simply furnished with pine; most have a balcony, all have a view. Your hosts, who come from Strasbourg, are lovely people who speak French and German (no English), and the food is good and local: sauerkraut and sausages, tarte flambé, gruyere and Munster cheese. Breads, jams and ice cream are all homemade. The Foessels know every mountain trail and their son is an off-piste guide, so tailored day trips are very much the thing. In early summer the meadows are sweet with flowers, there's a pretty garden to relax in and a large terrace for breakfast feasts.

rooms	5: 1 twin, 1 triple, 3 quadruples.
price	Half-board €37–€44 p.p.
meals	Half-board only. Picnic lunch €9.
closed	Rarely.
directions	From Albertville, N90 for Moutiers to Aime; RD86 for La Côte d'Aime for 5km to Pré Berard. Chalet on right.

Bed & Breakfast

piste or lift	20km		A & M Foessel
cross-country trail	20km	tel	+33 (0)4 79 55 52 07
lift for bikes	20km	fax	+33 (0)4 79 55 52 07
village centre	5km	e-mail	carlines@free.fr
		web	carlines.free.fr/gb/index.html

Map 5 Entry 55

Yellow Stone Chalet
Bonconseil Station, 73640 Sainte Foy, Savoie, France

The views are sensational from wherever you are – in your room, the jacuzzi, or rolling in the snow after your sauna. The mountain-perched chalet has a blazing fire for winter nights and a long table with upholstered chairs for comfortably convivial meals. Big carpeted bedrooms have bath or shower rooms and huge beds. Choose a book from the galleried library above the lounge and catch the last of the sun's rays on the south-facing terrace, surf the globe in the spanking new computer room, fit in a pre-dinner dip in the indoor pool-with-a-view. After a hearty breakfast your Franco-American hostess will help you map out your day, be it hiking, mountain-lake fishing or enjoying the winter playground that is Val d'Isere. You are on the edge of the shepherds' hamlet of Le Monal (so unspoiled it's listed), deserted in winter, surrounded by untracked snow. Yellow Stone could be a catered chalet if you were to come with a party, otherwise it's first-class B&B – and there's gîte space for eight. Tignes and Val d'Isère are easily reached by car.

rooms	6 + 1: 3 doubles, 3 suites for 4. Gîte for 8.
price	€ 110–€ 165. Singles € 85–€ 125. Suites € 140–€ 195. Gîte € 785–€ 1,700 per week.
meals	Dinner € 29; book ahead.
closed	Never.
directions	From Bourg St Maurice, D902 for Val d'Isère. After La Thuile, left for Ste Foy station & follow signs.

Bed & Breakfast

	Nancy Tabardel & Jean Marc Fouquet	
tel	+33 (0)4 79 06 96 06	
fax	+33 (0)4 79 06 96 05	
e-mail	yellowstone@wanadoo.fr	
web	www.yellowstone-chalet.com	

piste or lift	20m
village centre	200m

Map 5   Entry 56

Chalet Alexandria
Sainte Foy, Savoie, France

For off-piste adventurers, the baby of the Savoyard ski resorts is unsurpassed; few are in on the secret, so the pistes remain powdery all day long. (And the lift passes are cheap.) This brand-new, luxury chalet is built in the Savoyard style using local stone and wood, its entrance at the back on the first floor. The owner is an interior designer so you get the best: a sitting/dining room with open-plan kitchen that sweeps to French windows and a balcony with views; deep, comfortable sofas spaced around a central open fire; bright rugs on heated floors; a fresh and airy feel. Every ground-floor bedroom has a door to the wooden balcony and jacuzzi: immerse yourself in bubbles as the falling snow dusts your head. The master bedroom sits under the eaves, with another balcony. Country pine beds with Savoyard hearts have extra cushions and generous throws, there are country chests and books and games. Discuss the day's exploits over homemade cakes at tea; or over a glass of champagne as you anticipate a four-course dinner with wines. Ski shop, restaurants and bar are on the spot.

rooms	Chalet for 4: 2 doubles, 2 twins.
price	£1,000-£1,800 per week.
	Winter: £400-£575 p.p. per week.
meals	Self-catering. Catered in winter.
closed	Rarely.
directions	From Bourg St Maurice, follow signs for Val d'Isere. At Ste Foy, left for station.

Self-catering/Catered

piste or lift	50m
cross-country trail	1km
lift for bikes	1km
village centre	50m

Fiona Lynch

tel	+44 (0)7092 000300 (mob)
fax	+44 (0)7092 000350
e-mail	ski@premiere-neige.com
web	www.premiere-neige.com

Map 5 Entry 57

Chalet Number One
La Masure, 73640 Sainte Foy, Savoie, France

Built in 1668, this is the oldest house in the hamlet – and the hamlet is
surrounded by some of the finest skiing in the world. Steep stone steps lead to the
front door; the kitchen and dining room are upstairs, the living room down –
warmly clad, deeply inviting, with red sofas, Persian rugs and wood-burning
stove. Halogen lighting creates shadows on the exposed stone, Rothko prints
embolden the walls, there are videos, music, DVDs, satellite TV. You have three
bedrooms on the ground floor, four more below, and you sleep under goosedown.
In the morning, be inspired to venture up into the mountains accompanied
(should you choose) by your British Snowboarding Champion – and, now, keen
skiing – hosts. And there's a free shuttle. Lloyd and Sarah are great company and
Sarah a terrific cook – their three courses with good wines are an extra reason to
come. For summer you have the whole of the Vanoise National Park for walking
and the biking is magnificent, with a thrilling downhill course for pros and first-
timers alike. Take a dip afterwards in the pool of the restaurant up the road.

rooms	7: 5 twins/doubles, 2 triples.
price	£55–£65.
	Winter £370–£525 p.p. per week.
meals	Picnic lunch £5. Dinner with wine & coffee, £17. Catered in winter.
closed	Rarely.
directions	N90 Albertville to Bourg St Maurice; signs for Val d'Isere. At Sainte Foy village, left for La Masure. Chalet 1.5km on right.

Bed & Breakfast/Catered

	Lloyd & Sarah Rogers	piste or lift	6km
tel	+33 (0)4 79 06 95 33	cross-country trail	7km
fax	+33 (0)4 79 06 98 50	lift for bikes	14km
e-mail	info@chaletnumberone.com	village centre	1.5km
web	www.chaletnumberone.com		

Map 5 Entry 58

Chalet Chevalier

Le Planay Dessous, 73640 Sainte Foy, Savoie, France

At the end of a long winding road this feels like the edge of the world. Chalet Chevalier is one of a sprinkling of buildings in an ancient hamlet; carved wooden balconies span old stones and the views are sensational. You enter the rambling farmhouse on different levels, but the sitting room is the lovely heart of the place – a trio of red sofas and a roaring fire. French windows open onto a terrace from where you watch the sun slip behind the glaciers at the end of the day. All is rustic within and delightful: exposed stone walls, old beams, alpine furniture old and new, the odd Persian rug. Bedrooms are big and fresh with new pine beds and stripey covers; each double has a balcony. Bathrooms sparkle with halogen downlighters. Jacqui's four-course dinners are fantastic – chicken with lemon and shallots, hot chocolate soufflé – and contribute hugely to the pleasure of staying here. (B&B guests may eat out or in; there are restaurants and bars a short drive away, in Sainte Foy.) Daryl is a keen skier and tells you all you need to know – and Toby the St Bernard is full of bounce!

rooms	5: 3 doubles, 2 triples.
price	€60. Winter: €470–€590 p.p. per week.
meals	Picnic lunch €8. Dinner with wine & coffee, €20. Catered in winter.
closed	Never.
directions	D902 Bourg St Maurice-Val d'Isère. 1.5km past Ste Foy, left at small sign for Le Planay; 4km up road. Park at end of village; walk down track; 2nd on left.

Bed & Breakfast/Catered

piste or lift	20km			Daryl & Jacqui Morris
cross-country trail	50m	tel		+33 (0)4 79 06 51 69
lift for bikes	15km	e-mail		chaletchevalier@free.fr
village centre	4km	web		www.chaletchevalier.com

Map 5 Entry 59

Le Manoir de Bellecombe
25 route de St Oyen, 73260 Aigueblanche, Savoie, France

The thick stone walls and small, stone-carved window frames of the 17th-century manor ensure the house stays cool in summer and warm in winter. This is a genuinely simple, basic place to stay, with charm. A splendidly worn, stone stair leads to spotless bedrooms: coloured vinyl covers the floors, beds are wrought-iron, wardrobes old pine. The wide and rambling corridors are decorated with baskets of dried flowers; the breakfast room has a white-washed vaulted ceiling. There's no lounge, but a couple of comfortable chairs in the dining room. In winter you have board games, maps and books; in summer, a mature garden that springs into flower. Well-travelled Henri has spent a lot of time in Asia. He speaks good English and couldn't be more helpful, happy for B&B guests to rustle up their own suppers in the kitchen. The nearest restaurant/bar is in the village, a 10-minute walk, and there's skiing at the purpose-built but appealingly traditional resort of Valmorel.

rooms	6: 3 twins/doubles, 3 triples.
price	€43–€54. Singles €32. Self-catering €1,500–€2,200 per week.
meals	Picnic lunch €8. Dinner €16. Option to self-cater.
closed	Rarely.
directions	From Albertville N90 exit Aigueblanche. Through village for St Oyen. B&B 1km, after r'bout, on left.

Bed & Breakfast/Self-catering

	Henri & Françoise Charlin	piste or lift	1.5km
tel	+33 (0)4 79 24 31 95	cross-country trail	1.5km
fax	+33 (0)4 79 24 31 25	lift for bikes	1km
e-mail	henri@manoir-de-bellecombe.com	village centre	1.5km
web	www.manoir-de-bellecombe.com		

Map 5 Entry 60

Le Yéti
73553 Méribel les Allues, Savoie, France

Le Yéti has quite a site. Perched at the top of Méribel 1600, a pole's throw from the Rond Point des Pistes, it is bliss for skiers. This is a luxurious chalet-hotel whose architects – with the 1992 winter Olympics in mind – incorporated white vaulted ceilings and huge windows into an otherwise traditional design. The superbly woody sitting room/bar is warmly lit with large table lamps on chests and tables – sink into a stylish sofa with a good book, sip a *vin chaud* in front of the fire. Upstairs, beautiful roomy bedrooms are clad in pine. A creamy carpet covers the floor, checked or striped curtains frame an expanse of glass, bathrooms shine. Balconies face south or west and have huge views; family suites have bunk beds for kids. In summer, laze by the pool with its sweeping views of the village, or set off for a round of golf; in winter, ski right to the terrace for a lunch of salad and meats grilled over a wood fire. Chefs change year on year but the food is very good. Frédéric is a ski instructor and mountain guide and he and wife Sophie have created an unusually atmospheric place to stay.

rooms	32: 21 twins/doubles, 2 triples, 4 quadruples, 1 suite, 4 suites for 4.
price	€146-€295. High season: half-board only, €98-€185 p.p. Family rooms from €52 p.p.
meals	Breakfast €16. Dinner €45.
closed	May-June; September-mid-December.
directions	From Moutiers to Méribel. There, left for Altiport. At end of road.

Hotel

piste or lift	50m	
cross-country trail	1km	
lift for bikes	1km	
village centre	1km	

		Frédéric St Guilhem
tel		+33 (0)4 79 00 51 15
fax		+33 (0)4 79 00 51 73
e-mail		welcome@hotel-yeti.com
web		www.hotel-yeti.com

Map 5 Entry 61

Chalet Raphael
Le Raffort, 73550 Méribel, Savoie, France

The small village lies in the middle of Europe's biggest ski arena. The English owner fell for this cluster of 200-year-old buildings, did them up, then moved in. Inside is a living area cosy with red sofas and yellow cushions, soft lights, kilims on tiles and a big log fire. Rough-plaster walls are decorated with snow scenes and a large mirror; behind heavy curtains, French windows lead to a small decked terrace and hot tub (bliss on a frosty night). For summer: a sloping grass garden, shaded by plum trees, dotted with wild flowers. Bedrooms are impeccable, dressed in soft, warm colours with wooden ceilings and rounded beams. Simple patterned duvets and throws cover the iron or pine beds, rag rugs lie on carpeted floors, framed posters decorate the walls. Bridget is a wonderful cook and dinner is a long, relaxed, candlelit affair. She has masses of local knowledge and is never too busy; she'll accompany you on the pistes and trails if you ask. The *télécabine* gets you to the centre of Méribel village in six minutes; a bar/restaurant is a step away. *Cookery courses held in summer.*

rooms	6: 2 doubles, 3 twins, 1 family.
price	€ 60.
	Winter: € 495–€ 975 p.p. per week.
meals	Picnic lunch € 4. Dinner with wine, € 20. Catered in winter.
closed	Rarely.
directions	From Moutiers to Méribel. 3km after Les Allues, right at sign for Le Raffort. Chalet in village centre.

Bed & Breakfast/Catered

	Bridget Daley	piste or lift	150m
tel	+33 (0)4 79 00 45 69	cross-country trail	1km
fax	+33 (0)4 79 00 45 69	lift for bikes	150m
e-mail	bridget@skimeribelchalet.com	village centre	1km
web	www.skimeribel.com		

Map 5   Entry 62

La Marmotte Penthouse

Batiment Le Grand Sud, 73120 Courchevel 1650, Savoie, France

A recent facelift from a local architect has added a sparkle to this chalet style apartment block in 70s satellite Courchevel 1650. Now the posh penthouse under the eaves has great views *and* stacks of style. Neutral coloured sofas, bright with plump cushions, seat up to 10 in the living/dining room; vast windows open onto one of two sunny balconies that look over the village below. Floors are brushed oak, the kitchen is brilliantly equipped, bath and shower rooms shine, a fruit basket awaits you on arrival. Bedrooms are compact but hugely comfortable, with chunky rafters in sloping ceilings, built-in wardrobes, fat white duvets, the best mattresses. Carpeting is in burgundy wool, curtains are crisp and contemporary. The master bedroom shares an east-facing balcony with the bunk-bedded room and a stunning view, the twin is on a cosy mezzanine that looks down onto the living room. You couldn't be better placed for 1650's shops and bars... and you are a ski-booted hop away from the most sophisticated, far-reaching and interlinked skiing in the Alps. *Secure garage.*

rooms	Duplex for 10: 1 double, 1 twin with pull-out single on mezzanine, 1 room with bunk, pull-out single & sofabed.
price	€800–€2,575 per week.
meals	Self-catering. Chef on demand.
closed	Rarely.
directions	From Moutiers, follow signs to Courchevel 1650. Batiment le Grand Sud signed left.

Self-catering

piste or lift	350m
cross-country trail	1.5km
lift for bikes	350m
village centre	250m

Iain Wightwick

tel	+44 (0)117 929 8281
fax	+44 (0)117 906 9788
e-mail	info@rentapent.com
web	www.rentapent.com

Map 5 Entry 63

Hôtel de la Croisette
Place du Forum, 73120 Courchevel 1850, Savoie, France

Bang in the centre of Courchevel 1850 – so posh the King of Spain has a place here. English owners Tim and Janie chose the hotel for its position on the piste, in this dedicated skiers' resort. So the bar is madly busy, serving coffee and lunchtime snacks for skiers – and stronger stuff for for apres-ski loungers – up until one in the morning. (Ask for a bedroom on the top floor if you like peace and quiet.) Bar Le Jump is a fun place to be, with its buzzing atmosphere and carved antique fireplaces from Afghanistan. Down the spiral staircase is the living room where comfy sofas are pulled around the fire, and tables and chairs dotted in alcoves around a second (smaller, quieter) bar. Bedrooms are not luxurious but have been recently done up, with russet carpets, painted wooden walls, simple metal furniture and shining bathrooms in white and blue. Double-glazed windows at the front slide open to a small balcony and an alpine view; rooms at the back are quieter. Sophisticated Courchevel lies outside the door, a free resort bus circulates until midnight, and fearsome pistes abound.

rooms	18 twins/doubles.
price	€128–€230.
meals	Bar snacks €5–€12. Restaurants nearby.
closed	May & September–November.
directions	From Moutiers, follow signs to Courchevel 1850. Right at La Croisette, hotel straight ahead.

Hotel

	Tim Elwes	
tel	+33 (0)4 79 08 09 00	
fax	+33 (0)4 79 08 35 58	
e-mail	hotel.croisette@wanadoo.fr	
web	www.hoteldelacroisette.com	

piste or lift	20m
cross-country trail	3km
lift for bikes	20m
village centre	10m

Map 5 Entry 64

Chalet Bartavelle
Le Cruet, 73550 Méribel, Savoie, France

The ancient farms and barns of Le Cruet are a reminder of rural France in this (mostly) English-owned valley; half of one of them has been transformed by Jerry and Bettina into a superbly run chalet. Pass the owners' apartment, up the wooden steps and into a comfortable and characterful place to stay. You have a long, modern dining table by a big log fire, blue sofas, red curtains and colourful cushions. French windows open to a small garden with fruit trees and essential vegetable patch – food plays a major role here. Jerry was Senior Chef at London's Oxo Tower and turns out some formidable dishes: sweet onion marmalade tart with melted roquefort cheese, roast fillet of salmon with pomme anna potatoes, chocolate soufflé with a chocolate and orange sauce. You may be inspired to join his cookery classes, individually-tailored and held each spring and autumn. Bedrooms are cosy and carpeted under their eaves, with soft duvets and faux-fur throws. Five minutes from lively Méribel, even closer to Les Allues, the skiing's an absolute dream and your hosts will transport you to the slopes.

rooms	Chalet for 6-8: 4 twins/doubles.
price	B&B €50-€80. Chalet per week: €1,000-€1,350; half-board €2,000-€2,500; self-catering €800-€1,000. Winter: €2,500-€6,000.
meals	Dinner with wine, €40; book ahead. Catered in winter.
closed	Rarely.
directions	2km past Méribel les Allues, right for Vanthier. 1st on left.

Self-catering/Catered/B&B

piste or lift	1.5km
cross-country trail	2km
lift for bikes	1.5km
village centre	1.5km

	Jerry & Bettina Mant
tel	+33 (0)4 79 08 19 55
fax	+33 (0)4 79 08 19 55
e-mail	chaletbartavelle@wanadoo.fr
web	www.chalet-bartavelle-meribel.co.uk

Map 5 Entry 65

La Maison du Villard
Hameau le Villard, 73500 Saint André, Savoie, France

The heart swells with pleasure as you arrive at this old farmhouse on the edge of the Vanoise National Park. The hamlet, 1,300m up near the Italian border – and five miles from the nearest lift that takes you into the Trois Vallées terrain – looks across the valley to mountain peaks. Charming Bernard is a qualified summer and winter guide, and he and Michelle know all there is to know about summer hikes, and springtime snowshoe treks in search of wildlife and rare flowers. A delicious hamper will be packed before you set off, and you can go with Bernard or on your own. In winter there's skiing and *ski de fond* at Aussois, La Norma, Orelle. Bedrooms are modest but large, with just the odd piece of country furniture, a few books and maps. Le Villard is genuine, unpretentious, a friendly family house perfect for active types who also love good food and company. There are restaurants four miles away at Modane, but dinners here, in the vaulted cellar, are jolly affairs, followed by stories around the open fire, board games, perhaps a glass of genepi. In summer parasoled tables dot the toy-strewn lawn.

rooms	6: 4 twins, 1 triple, 1 quadruple.
price	€50–€60. Suites €90–€120. Full-board €52 p.p.
meals	Picnic lunch €4–€6. Dinner €15.
closed	Never.
directions	Exit A43 Modane for Saint André; right for Hameau le Villard. B&B on left at village entrance.

Bed & Breakfast

	Michelle & Bernard Trigon
tel	+33 (0)4 79 05 27 17
fax	+33 (0)4 79 05 27 17
e-mail	lamaisonduvillard@wanadoo.fr
web	www.maisonduvillard.com

piste or lift	8km
cross-country trail	15km
lift for bikes	15km
village centre	7km

Map 5 Entry 66

Les Méans
04340 Méolans Revel, Alpes-de-Haute-Provence, France

Beds are just for sleeping here. The beauty of the place will have you up and over the mountains before breakfast, and Fréderic is a qualified guide. Being so near the Ubaye river, rafting, canoeing and kayaking are on the agenda, too. The Millets lead double lives: ski instructors in the winter (when the B&B closes), hospitable hosts in the summer. Their farmhouse is 16th-century, delightful inside, and, with communal washing machines, microwave, kettle and fridge packed with soft drinks, brilliant for families. There's also an honesty bar and coffee on tap all day. Elizabeth cooks on the roasting-spit three nights a week – pigeon is one of her specialities – and you eat in the big, white, vaulted dining room that opens to the kitchen. Once the sheepfold, it now brims beautifully with baskets, drying herbs and colourful odds and ends. There are checked sofas and an open fire in the sitting room, a hot tub on the terrace, mountain gazing from the garden. Stir yourself to visit the hamlet's chapel, and note the bread oven in the garden, cleverly restored by Fréderic.

rooms	5: 4 doubles, 1 suite for 2-4.
price	€60-€85. Suites €95-€140.
meals	Dinner with wine & coffee, €22-€25; 3 days a week. Restaurant 5km.
closed	Mid-October-mid-April.
directions	D900 Gap-Barcelonnette. 10km from Lauzet-Ubaye, after La Fresquière, ignore right turn for Méolans. B&B 500m further on left.

Bed & Breakfast

piste or lift	20km		Elisabeth Millet	
cross-country trail	10km	tel	+33 (0)4 92 81 03 91	
lift for bikes	20km	fax	+33 (0)4 92 81 03 91	
village centre	5km	e-mail	lesmeans@chez.com	
		web	www.chez.com/lesmeans	

Map 5 Entry 67

Chalet Lavis Trafford
Le Planay, 73500 Bramans, Savoie, France

Open all year, but only get-at-able by horse and sleigh in winter! In fact, the track is suitable for cars only between May and October: the rest of the year you ski cross-country or take that sleigh. (Walking takes 45 minutes; phone ahead and they'll fetch your bags.) The chalet snuggles deep in a larched forest with only wildlife for company: not a whisper but the falling snow. It was used by farmers in the old days when livestock was moved up to the high pastures, and is enchanting in summer, too. The old wooden façade is beautifully weathered and the stone lauze of the roof is gathering moss. Cosy rooms are clad with darkened larch, brought to life by the red and white of gingham in curtains and spreads. The living room has a patterned sofa and new pine, there are soft lights and an open fire. Delicious food comes in generous quantities, with a wide range of local specialities. Peaceful walks and cross-country or snowshoe trails abound, there are glaciers and lakes to discover, and you can paraglide or go canyoneering in summer. Let François be your guide. An amazing hideaway.

rooms	5: 4 doubles, 1 quadruple.
price	€ 68.
meals	Picnic lunch € 10. Dinner € 17.
closed	April; mid-November-mid-December.
directions	N6 Bramans; D100 for Le Planay. Chalet on left after bridge. In winter, park at Bramans; bus to Notre Dame de la Deliverance; 3km by foot or sleigh.

Bed & Breakfast

	François & Florence de Grolée	
tel	+33 (0)4 79 05 06 83	
e-mail	info@chalet-lavis-trafford.com	
web	www.chalet-lavis-trafford.com	

cross-country trail	10m
lift for bikes	15km
village centre	7km

Map 5 Entry 68

Solneige
Lieu-dit de Pourchery, 38114 Vaujany, Isère, France

An 1891 farmhouse turned B&B in a gem of a village. Rooms blend old and new beautifully – very Dutch – and the French/Italian food is delicious. Bedrooms have the original balconies and shutters while tiles and 17th-century-style fireplaces are new, and an open-air whirlpool and sauna are planned. Meals are lively, at a long table by candlelight, a simple chandelier floating from a white vaulted ceiling. Bedrooms have neutral colours, iron beds, crisp bed linen, vases of flowers and translucent curtains that flutter in the breeze. The look is stylishly contemporary – two retrievers and five cats add a homely touch. In the modern kitchen, ingeniously incorporated into a cloister with an arched ceiling, Jan and Mirjam prepare breakfasts as generous as their evening meals; they also offer a shuttle service to the pistes. Vaujany has kept its old-world charm in spite of the demands of skiers; there's a new sports centre and a 160-person cable car to ship you up to the vast Alpe d'Huez. In spring, the snows give way to goats, hens and drifts of wild flowers.

rooms	5 + 2: 1 double, 2 twins, 2 triples; 2 apartments for 6.
price	€56. Apartments €370–€520 p.w. Winter €412–€512 p.p. p.w.; apartments €688–€1,042 per week.
meals	Picnic lunch €6. Dinner €22.50. Catered in winter.
closed	May & October-November.
directions	N91 Grenoble-Briançon; 18km; left for Vaujany. On rt at village entrance.

Bed & Breakfast/Catered

piste or lift	2.5km	Jan & Mirjam Dekker de Wilde
cross-country trail	2.5km	tel +33 (0)4 76 79 88 18
lift for bikes	2.5km	e-mail solneige@planet.nl
village centre	2.5km	web www.solneige.com

Map 5   Entry 69

Florineige
Quartier de la Fruitière, 38750 Huez en Oisans, Isère, France

The village is a hillside collection of old stone houses with steeply-pitched roofs and meandering streets. There's an old church and a brand-new gondola – sweeping you up to adventures on the Alpe d'Huez. Sylvie and Yves have incorporated a warm, simple guesthouse into their home, where open-stone walls and reclaimed larch panelling has been brought to life with bright fabrics, paper lamps and new wooden floors. Furniture is a mix of Savoyard and velveteen-modern. Breakfast is a hearty affair that includes homemade jams, baguettes and local yogurt; supper is taken over the road in their hotel – an indulgence of French and regional specialities. Yves is a ski instructor in winter and a mountaineer in summer, and both he and Sylvie are a friendly mine of information. Bedrooms are as neat as apple pie: new pine beds are dressed in red, check curtains frame wooden windows. Two of the rooms look onto the lovely enclosed garden (perfect for children in summer), the others have mountain or village views. A delight.

rooms	4: 1 double, 3 quadruples.
price	€51-€71. Half-board €38-€51 p.p.
meals	Half-board option (dinner) in hotel opposite (entry 71).
closed	Rarely.
directions	From Grenoble A480 exit 8 for Vizille les Stations de l'Oisans; N91 to Bourg d'Oisans; left on CD211 for Alpe d'Huez. Huez en Oisans 4km before Alpe d'Huez.

Bed & Breakfast

	Yves & Sylvie Forestier	
tel	+33 (0)4 76 80 94 89	
e-mail	forestieryves@aol.com	
web	www.hebergement-florineige.com	

piste or lift	150m
cross-country trail	3km
lift for bikes	150m
village centre	10m

Map 5 Entry 70

Hôtel L'Ancolie
Avenue de l'Eglise, 38750 Huez en Oisans, Isère, France

Yves and Sylvie had long wanted to open a proper hotel in Huez en Oisans – and now they have. They've been part of this tight-knit community since 1995: started off with *chambre d'hôtes* (see previous entry), then took on a wreck of an old farmhouse down the road, did it up and topped it with a fine larch roof. The result is a simple, delightful place to stay. Some of the bedrooms have chunky ceiling beams, others exposed stone walls, while the cosiest are under the eaves. Furniture is plain modern pine with the odd rustic chest. The light-filled restaurant serves local specialities as well as French dishes before an open fire; French windows open to a sunny terrace in summer and extravagant views. From Easter on the village thrums with cyclists intent on one on the most famous ascents of the Alps; Yves is a mountain biker and can take you on a guided tour. (In winter he swaps wheels for poles and skis.) The charming little village of Huez is a short cable car ride to glorious skiing at Alpe d'Huez.

rooms	16: 14 twins/doubles, 1 triple, 1 quadruple.
price	€64-€102.
meals	Breakfast €6. Dinner €20-€30.
closed	Mid-April-June; September-mid-December.
directions	From Grenoble, A480 exit 8 for Vizille-Les Stations de'Oisans; N91 to Bourg d'Oisans; left on CD211 for Alpe d'Huez. Huez en Oisans 4km before resort.
Hotel	

piste or lift	150m		Yves & Sylvie Forestier	
cross–country trail	3km	tel	+33 (0)4 76 11 13 13	
lift for bikes	150m	fax	+33 (0)4 76 11 13 11	
village centre	10m	e-mail	Forestieryves@aol.com	
		web	www.hebergement-florineige.com	

Map 5 Entry 71

La Roche Meane
Villar d'Arene, 05480 La Grave, Hautes-Alpes, France

Narrow streets branch out from the 17th-century church and village square –
then it's five minutes to La Roche Meane. A few years ago your hosts turned the
old stone barn into a B&B and happy family home. Doing much of the work
themselves, Xavier and Sylviane left no old stone unexposed; the result is a
delightfully unpretentious place to stay. There's no sitting room or room for
evening meals, but there is a good clutch of restaurants and bars around the
square. And you can use their kitchen if you like. Come in autumn for golden
leaves and snow dusting the peaks of the Ecrins National Park, in winter, for some
of the most dazzling off-piste skiing in the world. It's five minutes by car to La
Grave, then lifts to the wide and not too terrifying slopes of Les Deux Alpes
(dubbed by snowboarders as L2A). In spring, streams turn to torrents as the snow
retreats and the hillsides burst into flower; in summer Xavier, a trained guide,
takes you on hikes to high pastures. A spiral stone stair with a rope banister leads
to simple bedrooms under the eaves. Charming, and great value.

rooms	5: 3 twins, 1 triple, 1 quadruple.
price	€42–€88.
meals	Restaurants in village.
closed	Rarely.
directions	From Briancon, N91 over Col du Lautaret to Villar d'Arene. Park in village square.

Bed & Breakfast

	Xavier & Sylviane Cret
tel	+33 (0)4 76 79 91 43
fax	+33 (0)4 76 79 91 43
e-mail	rochemeane@wanadoo.fr
web	www.rochemeane.com

piste or lift	2.5km
cross-country trail	10m
lift for bikes	2.5km
village centre	10m

Map 5 Entry 72

Hôtel Alliey
Serre-Chevalier, 05220 Monêtier les Bains, Hautes-Alpes, France

An old stone mountain house – or rather two – transformed into a traditional, family-friendly hotel in cobbled Monêtier les Bains. Once it was a modest spa village, now it has lifts that whisk you into the winter wonderworld that is Serre Chevalier. (In summer there's the Ecrins National Park.) The hotel sits surrounded by Monêtier's 16th-century chapel, market square and lively restaurants and shops. Hervé Buisson is a mountain man with a love of country cooking and a passion for wine – his cellar sports 10,000 bottles – so you are well looked after: rack of lamb with herbs, white trout on a compote of leeks, flavoursome local cheeses. The restaurant is cosy with panelled walls and little windows hung with lace, there are red and white gingham cloths on simple tables, and an open fire in the corner. Bedrooms are utilitarian but comfortable with beige carpeting, patterned curtains and new pine. Two swimming pools (one in, one out), a spa, early meals for children, loan of bottle heaters and cots, babysitting on request: it's wonderful for families.

rooms	39: 24 twins/doubles, 15 suites for 3-4.
price	Half-board €61-€82 p.p. Suites half-board €75-€92 p.p.
meals	Half-board only.
closed	May-mid-June; mid September-mid-December.
directions	14km from Briançon on N91. In village centre, on left, near church.
Hotel	

piste or lift	350m		Eliane & Hervé Buisson
cross-country trail	500m	tel	+33 (0)4 92 24 44 20
lift for bikes	350m	fax	+33 (0)4 92 24 40 60
village centre	10m	e-mail	hotel@alliey.com
		web	www.alliey.com

Map 5 Entry 73

L'Auberge du Choucas
Monêtier les Bains, 05220 Serre Chevalier, Hautes-Alpes, France

In an eternity of blue skies and glacial peaks, revelling in sunshine 300 days a year, is this delightful old inn. It's right in the middle of the ancient spa village, tucked behind the romanesque church, surrounded by ski slopes and ice caves, long walks and hot springs. The auberge's garden is made for summer breakfasts with the birds, the sitting room for cosy fireside teas, and the stone-vaulted dining room with its great open fire is a fitting setting for some superb food from a young chef. "The art of cookery has been lifted into the realm of poetry," gushed one guest. There's art on the walls and the bedroom doors have been beautifully painted by an artist friend. Bedrooms are wood-panelled, carpeted and cottagey, with snug little bathrooms. Those with balconies catch the morning sun; two-floor duplexes have two bathrooms. It's a terrific place, masterminded by the whirlwind Nicole, who also nutures a passion for Latin and Greek. Along with her charming daughter, Eva, she tends to the minutest detail, keen that all should be perfect.

rooms	12: 8 twins/doubles, 4 duplexes for 2-4.
price	Half-board €100-€230.
meals	Breakfast €15. Lunch €19-€39. Dinner €29-€60. Restaurant closed mid-April-May; mid-October-mid-December.
closed	May; 3 Nov-6 Dec.
directions	From Briançon on N91. In centre, behind church, in front of town hall.

Hotel

	Nicole Sanchez-Ventura	piste or lift	300m
tel	+33 (0)4 92 24 42 73	cross-country trail	1km
fax	+33 (0)4 92 24 51 60	lift for bikes	300m
e-mail	auberge.du.choucas@wanadoo.fr	village centre	10m
web	www.aubergeduchoucas.com		

Map 5   Entry 74

Les Marmottes
22 rue du Centre, Chantemerle, St Chaffrey, 05330 Serre Chevalier, Hautes-Alpes, France

You can't miss the butter-yellow walls of this big old house on the edge of the village. Up the stone steps, through the heavy pine door and Denis or Karin are there to greet you – he a ski instructor, she, English, in charge of B&B. They are the nicest, kindest hosts, and live in a separate apartment in the building. The focus of the ancient-beamed sitting room is the traditional open fire with its vast pine-clad chimney breast. A sawn-off beer barrel serves as a coffee table, there's a warm red rug and three great white sofas to sink into. Upstairs is an equally snug breakfast and dining room, where you feast upon good, regional dishes. From here a corridor leads to a couple of the bedrooms; the rest are up a second flight of stairs. The rooms – simple, light and clean – are named after a mountain, a resort or an alpine sport; floors are wooden, bath and shower rooms colourfully tiled. The village of Chantemerle ('singing blackbird') is as pretty as its name and you are in the middle of it – minutes from the shops and the cable car to Grand Alpe. A peaceful, welcoming place.

rooms	4 twins/doubles.
price	€ 74–€ 112. Half-board € 56–€ 75 p.p.
meals	Dinner € 19. High season half-board only.
closed	Rarely.
directions	From Briancon, N91 to Chantemerle. 1st left on entering village. Chalet 200m on left, 100m from church.

Bed & Breakfast

piste or lift	200m	Denis & Karin Lucas
cross-country trail	1km	tel +33 (0)4 92 24 11 17
lift for bikes	200m	fax +33 (0)4 92 24 11 17
village centre	100m	e-mail lucas@marrmottes@wanadoo.fr

Map 5 Entry 75

Chalet St Clair
St Chaffrey, Hautes-Alpes, France

The charming little village of St Chaffrey lies on sunny, south-facing slopes; its streets (shop, post office, bar) radiate from a 12th-century chapel. The chalet itself is younger (late 1700s). It was a ruin for half a century; now it's a superb little guesthouse. Earthen floors have been replaced by polished timber and underfloor heating, there's a whitewashed, vaulted ceiling, lots of exposed stone and lights sunk into the floor – a luxurious, cosy, modern-rustic feel. The original metal hooks for agriculturial implements remain, there are designer paper lamps, fine Scandinavian furniture, glossy English magazines, perfectly-placed rows of framed prints. You dine at a large wooden table; Hanna is from Sweden and once a week dreams up a Nordic speciality. Bedrooms vary in size and look and are fresh with modern pine; there's a mattress in a tiny fourth room for an extra child. Graham is a ski instructor so you are in good hands, and the ski lifts are at Chantemerle, a five-minute drive by bus or navette.

rooms	3: 1 family room (for 4), 2 twins.
price	€ 50–€ 70.
meals	Picnic lunch € 8. Dinner with wine, € 16.
closed	Rarely.
directions	From Briançon, N91 for St Chaffrey. Approx. 5km from resort, signed right to village, right before raising bridge. Chalet on left.

Bed & Breakfast

	Graham & Hanna Sinclair	
tel	+33 (0)4 92 24 23 34	
fax	+44 (0)1534 483859	
e-mail	chalet.st.clair@free.fr	
web	www.chaletstclair.co.uk	

piste or lift	1.5km
cross-country trail	1.5km
lift for bikes	1.5km
village centre	200m

Map 5 Entry 76

Photography by Tim Brook

switzerland

Chalet Les Papillons
Arveyes, 1884 Villars, Switzerland

Life-sized replicas of red toy trains trundle past every so often, tooting as they go. The mountain railway has a small hop-on-and-off point just above the chalet – so you can pop down roughly once an hour. (The family also have a minibus which they use for ferrying guests.) Véronique and Jean-Pierre, their three children and their bouncy dog, enjoy sharing their home with guests. There's a small breakfast room whose French windows open to a sunny terrace, and four simple, carpeted bedrooms. Les Sapins has green curtains embroided with Christmas trees; le Lac, the triple, hides darkly under the wooded eaves, its curtains dotted with edelweiss. Furniture is wicker and pine. You get wonderful homemade bread and local honey and jams at breakfast; lunches will be at mountain restaurants, dinner down in Villars. It's a bustling little place, popular with the Brits and good news for families. Back in your mountain hideaway, the children can play in the garden with swings, as you admire the views. Villars is delightful – a well-kept secret.

rooms	4: 1 double, 2 twins, 1 triple.
price	Chf100-Chf140.
meals	Restaurants 1km.
closed	Never.
directions	From Aigle, signs to Villars; on 1.5km to Gryon; B&B on left, above railway line.

Bed & Breakfast

piste or lift	1.5km
cross-country trail	1.5km
lift for bikes	1.5km
village centre	1.5km

		Véronique de Guigné
tel		+41 (0)24 495 3484
fax		+41 (0)24 495 4231
e-mail		v.guigne@bluewin.ch

Map 5 Entry 77

Hôtel La Renardière
1884 Villars, Switzerland

Yves is director at the tourist office, so you'll not run out of things to do! The Defalques took on the three-chalet hotel (linked by covered passageways) and spruced it up from top to toe. A drive through well-kept gardens brings you to the front door. To the left of reception is the sitting room: panelled pine, open fire, red and green sofas, grand piano and doors leading in summer to the garden. Bedrooms upstairs are knotted-pine-panelled, have pale carpets and gorgeous floral curtains with bedside lamps to match. Old-fashioned iron radiators belt out the heat; French windows open to balconies (most of the rooms have them), bathrooms have thick towels and tempting toiletries. It's all so warm and easy you could be staying with friends. You get freshly squeezed orange juice and croissants for breakfast; supper in the woody restaurant is candlelit with a good choice of dishes. Villars, reached by winding road or quaint mountain railway, is a great family resort all year; lucky you to be in the heart of it.

rooms	17 + 2: 13 twins/doubles, 2 quadruples, 2 triples. 2 apartments: 1 for 2, 1 for 4.
price	€ 165–€ 320. Singles € 113–€ 193. Apartments € 310–€ 580.
meals	Half-board option: extra € 30 p.p.
closed	Rarely.
directions	From Aigle, follow signs to Villars. In village centre, left for Les Diablerets. Hotel 150m on left, set back from road.
Hotel	

	Yves Defalque	piste or lift	300m
tel	+41 (0)24 495 25 92	cross-country trail	200m
fax	+41 (0)24 495 39 15	lift for bikes	300m
e-mail	info@larenardiere.ch	village centre	200m
web	www.larenardiere.ch		

Map 5   Entry 78

Hotel La Rocaille
1660 Château d'Oex, Switzerland

It's a hot-air ballooning outpost, this – once the launch pad for the Breitling Orbitor's record-breaking ride around the globe. Ann and Patrik took over La Rocaille 10 years ago, started a family, and have worked hard to create this warm and friendly place to stay. The chalet rests at the end of the high street in the small but perfectly formed village of Château d'Oex. Inside there's a pleasing mood of stylish rusticity. Quarry tiles, halogen-lit modern art on the walls, a breakfast buffet groaning with local cheeses, fruits and homemade breads and jams. Big windows pull in the light and the village views. Downstairs is a small beamed stübe with open fire and pretty, new furniture. Bedrooms have white walls, wooden ceilings, elegant wrought-iron beds with lamps to match, more modern art; all are different, all (bar one) have their own bathrooms. Patrik conjures up flavoursome and good-looking dishes in the kitchen, and uses the freshest produce.

rooms	12: 9 twins/doubles, 3 suites for 4.
price	Chf140-Chf210. Singles Chf90-Chf140.
meals	Dinner Chf35.
closed	October-November.
directions	Exit A12 Bulle to Gruyères & on for 25km; left to Château d'Oex & along high street. Hotel 200m after centre, on right.

Hotel

piste or lift	1.5km	
cross-country trail	1km	
lift for bikes	1.5km	
village centre	200m	

Ann & Patrik Gazeau
tel	+41 (0)26 924 6215
fax	+41 (0)26 924 5249
e-mail	rocaille@swissonline.ch
web	www.larocaille.ch

Map 6 Entry 79

Le Vieux Chalet
1660 Château d'Oex, Switzerland

Charlene came from Chicago, fell in love with the village and one of its residents, then married him. Together they bought a 19th-century guesthouse on the edge of town and turned it into a little school; two decades on, the classroom across the drive is a games room with a basketball hoop and table tennis. Le Vieux Chalet is still perfect for children. Inside, dark half-panelling lines reception, a table is laid with leaflets about the area, and the sitting room is rustically furnished with a homely feel. Up the wooden stairs are the guestrooms, modestly but comfortably furnished with old wrought-iron or pine-boat beds. Walls are pine-clad, carpets green, top-floor rooms nicely beamed. Ask for a room with a balcony so you can sit and watch the hot-air balloons rise from the valley and drift off into the blue beyond (Château d'Oex is a hotbed of enthusiasts). Jean Bach and his son are ski instructors – perfect. It's a short stroll to the village for dinner, and there's a little kitchen should you prefer to cook your own. *Whole chalet available for self-catering.*

rooms	18: 6 twins/doubles, 6 triples, 5 family rooms, 1 dorm for 5.
price	Chf90-Chf100.
meals	Dinner Chf35 (for groups of 20+).
closed	Never.
directions	Leave A12 at Bulle for Gruyères; 25km; left to Château d'Oex. 1st left for La Frasse. B&B 200m on left.

Bed & Breakfast/Self-catering

	Jean Bach	piste or lift	1km
tel	+41 (0)26 924 6879	cross-country trail	400m
fax	+41 (0)26 924 4311	lift for bikes	1km
e-mail	vieuxchalet@bluewin.ch	village centre	400m

Map 6 Entry 80

Posthotel Rössli
3780 Gstaad, Switzerland

It's tough keeping up with the mink coats and Mercedes of ritzy Gstaad: social life here is by invite only. Dare to be different and stay in one of the least swanky hotels in town. Through the carved door to the panelled restaurant and bar, humming with locals from morning till night; then up the creaking stair to the reception and guest bedrooms. These come panelled in mellow old pine, have good beds and a traditional feel; newer rooms may be shorter on character but are carpeted and comfortable and have super bath and shower rooms. Food is traditional Swiss and in summer the restaurant spills into a fruit-treed garden. On the pedestrianised high street, this is the oldest hostelry in town, in Ruedi's family for over 80 years. A keen alpine climber and skier in his youth, Ruedi still guides in summer, and, given a little encouragement, will regale you with stories over a stein of beer. The resort, in spite of its chic-ness, is smaller than most, and deeply traditional. Rejoice that you are in the traffic-free heart of it. *Ask for details of special deals.*

rooms	18 twins/doubles.
price	Chf180–Chf340.
meals	Dinner Chf33.
closed	April–May.
directions	In centre of Gstaad.

Hotel

piste or lift	500m		Ruedi Widmer	
cross–country trail	500m	tel	+41 (0)33 748 4242
lift for bikes	500m	fax	+41 (0)33 748 4243
village centre	10m	e–mail	info@posthotelroessli.ch
		web	www.posthotelroessli.ch

Map 6   Entry 81

Landgasthof Ruedihus
3718 Kandersteg, Switzerland

The façade is astonishing. Exquisite pine carved two centuries ago, with the dark patina of age, and strikingly fine latticed windows. Duck into a low-ceilinged stübe, cosy with floral curtains, dried flowers in copper pots and 1920s-style lamps suspended above tables. The dining room is smarter, with crisp white napery and curtains to match. Delicious smells of fondues and raclettes emanate from a kitchen that serves creative but traditional Swiss dishes; a carved wooden stair with beautiful worn banister transports you to bed. Rooms vary in size, some large, others tucked under the eaves. All are immaculately carpeted and furnished with repro pieces, maybe an antique or a four-poster. Those with the original windows are dimly lit. This charming old hotel does not have the swish facilities of its young sister hotel the Dolderhorn, but in summer it's a five-minute stroll to whirlpool, sauna and spa. A dry-stone wall guards a magnificent organic vegetable garden at the front, and you have a pretty, white-parasoled terrace.

rooms	10: 8 twins/doubles, 1 single, 1 suite.
price	Chf200-Chf220. Singles Chf100-Chf150. Suites Chf230-Chf260.
meals	Dinner Chf45.
closed	Never.
directions	From Spiez, follow signs to Kandersteg. Hotel at far end of village, set back on right.

Hotel

	René & Anne Maeder
tel	+41 (0)33 675 8181
fax	+41 (0)33 675 8185
e-mail	doldenhorn@compuserve.com
web	www.doldenhorn-ruedihus.ch

piste or lift	1.5km
cross-country trail	1.5km
lift for bikes	1.5km
village centre	1.5km

Map 6 Entry 82

Waldhotel Doldenhorn
3718 Kandersteg, Switzerland

Cross-country skiers are in heaven here. The trails go far – and the terrain for beginner-downhillers is also first-rate. The Langasthof Ruedihus's sister hotel has been immaculately built, and, thanks to the Maeders, runs on particularly well-oiled wheels. You have a trio of restaurants: charming stübe for local dishes, gourmet room with chandelier, and airy, white *wintergarten* with a terrace for summer. A feast of pale pine soaring into the rafters is the living room… a mezzanine above, a grand piano by the bar, checked sofas, an open fire. Bedrooms are hotel-comfy and furniture the best reproduction mahogany. Carpets are neutral or blue, generous curtains frame big, light-filled windows. Rooms under the eaves have an additional mezzanine, all have a seating area, and most a west-facing balcony to catch the evening sun. The sumptuous wellness centre has steam, sauna, jacuzzi and gym, and opens to a meadow-like garden sprinkled wth loungers. One more reason to come here is the village: charming Kandersteg is lined with cuckoo-clock houses.

rooms	60: 52 twins/doubles, 6 suites, 2 family rooms.
price	Chf200-Chf310. Singles Chf110-Chf220. Suites Chf300-Chf600.
meals	Dinner Chf45.
closed	Never.
directions	From Spiez, follow signs to Kandersteg. Hotel at far end of village, set back on left.

Hotel

piste or lift	1.5km		René & Anne Maeder
cross-country trail	1.5km	tel	+41 (0)33 675 8181
lift for bikes	1.5km	fax	+41 (0)33 675 8185
village centre	1.5km	e-mail	doldenhorn@compuserve.com
		web	www.doldenhorn-ruedihus.ch

Map 6 Entry 83

Olle & Maria's B&B
Nidrimatten, Gimmelwald, 3826 Mürren, Switzerland

The ascent is sheer – and stunning. Once you've recovered from the view, step out of the cable car to a row of chocolate-box chalets on a tiny street. Olle and Maria's was once a farmhouse, now it's home to two teachers, three children, a cat and B&B guests. The open-plan living/dining/kitchen area has a smouldering winter fire, soaring views, and wood, wood everywhere – the built-in benches, the table, the cupboards, the chests stocked with books and games. Upstairs is a pine-clad, slopey-ceilinged bedroom for you – a pine bed, a blue-and-green painted wardrobe in the corner, white curtains at the window, a rug, some books. The cork-floored bathroom, sparklingly modern, is shared with the family. Olle and Maria also have a small apartment for guests downstairs, with its own entrance: fresh white walls, a wooden ceiling, a kitchenette, a little private terrace with more views – all you need. (And they'll do you breakfast if you like.) They are good people – elated to have swapped a guesthouse in Bern for alpine pastures and clunking cow bells.

rooms	1 + 1: 1 double sharing family bathroom. 1 apartment for 3.
price	Chf110–Chf180.
meals	Breakfast Chf18. Restaurant nearby.
closed	Never.
directions	Continue past Lauterbrunnen & park at Stechleberg cable-car; 1st stage to Gimmelwald. B&B a 5-minute walk, on left.

Bed & Breakfast/Self-catering

	Olle & Maria Eggimann	piste or lift	300m
tel	+41 (0)33 855 3575	cross-country trail	10m
e-mail	oeggimann@bluewin.ch	lift for bikes	300m
		village centre	10m

Map 6 Entry 84

Hotel Jungfrau & Haus Mönch
3825 Mürren, Switzerland

By sparkling gondola or rickety train – however you get here, the ride will be glorious. Andres and Anne-Marie have run guesthouses in Mürren (car-free, absurdly pretty) for years. Flags of all nations flutter outside the Jungfrau. In their capable hands since 2000, it's a friendly yet stylish place with an international appeal; even Aussies join the fans. The main hotel sits next to the ski school, its terrace sweeping onto the slopes; Haus Mönch is the annexe across the lane. Pull up an armchair in front of the living room's log fire, borrow book or board games (many are in English) from the reading room next door. Upstairs are the bedrooms, light and airy with balconies and beautiful views. Plain-carpeted, softly-lit, with fresh white walls and crisp bedlinen, they have a delightful feel. Dine on seasonal, regional dishes in the Restaurant Gruebi – as you watch beginners taking a tumble on the nursery slopes outside. The high altitude guarantees snow-clad rooftops and trees; in summer, take a trip up to the revolving restaurant at Piz Gloria, or spin off on bikes. Every season here is a joy.

rooms	47: 19 doubles, 6 singles, 4 triples. Haus Mönch: 18 twins/doubles.
price	Chf170-Chf290. Haus Mönch Chf 70-Chf100.
meals	Dinner Chf25-Chf55.
closed	May & October-November.
directions	Park in Lauterbrunnen & take train to Mürren, then electric taxi for luggage. Hotel 5-minute walk from station.

Hotel

piste or lift	100m
cross-country trail	2km
village centre	10m

Andres & Anne-Marie Goetschi

tel	+41 (0)33 855 4545
fax	+41 (0)33 855 4549
e-mail	mail@hoteljungfrau.ch
web	www.hoteljungfrau.ch

Map 6 Entry 85

Hotel Regina
3823 Wengen, Switzerland

Grand and old-fashioned – just like Wengen. A beautiful red train cranks you up the mountain to the perched village, an electric car spins you to the hotel. Come for deep comfort and good food. You get two restaurants, one rustic, one gourmet: Chez Meyers, its warm yellow walls dotted with Victorian black and white portraits, serves local specialities; the Grand Restaurant, all arch-topped windows and magnificent views, does five-course international. Retire with coffee or cognac to a fireside snug in the sitting room, dominated by its ornately carved 1894 stone fireplace crackling with logs. Kilims soften the gleaming wooden floors, the glow of the table lamps adds to the London-club atmosphere. Guestrooms, too, take one back to a gentler age, with their mahogany beds, floral drapes and leather-bound wallets (packed with local information). Guido and Ariane are lovely genuine people; they and their staff have created a sedately special place to stay. Car-free Wengen lies at your door. *Ask for details of all-inclusive summer/winter deals.*

rooms	90: 72 twins/doubles, 14 singles, 4 suites.
price	Chf270-Chf500.
meals	Chf78 or à la carte.
closed	Mid-April-May; mid-October-November.
directions	A car free resort. Park in Lauterbrunnen, & take train to Wengen. Call ahead & hotel will arrange transport from station.

Hotel

	Guido & Ariane Meyer	piste or lift	150m
tel	+41 (0)33 856 5858	cross-country trail	400m
fax	+41 (0)33 856 5850	lift for bikes	150m
e-mail	regina@wengen.com	village centre	100m
web	www.wengen.com/regina		

Map 6 Entry 86

Hotel Falken
3823 Wengen, Switzerland

Take the world's quaintest mountain railway to Wengen and head straight for the Falkan. (You'd be hard-pushed to get here any other way: Wengen and Mürren are virtually traffic-free.) A period piece, and in the same family for years, it has long been an English favourite; indeed, the feel is more Edwardian than Tyrolean. The lounge, patterned-carpet-cosy, is filled with velvety fauteuils; the dining room, with bentwood chairs at white-clothed tables, is charming. Historic photographs, paintings by local artists and cushions embroidered by former guests add to the homely feel. And there's a music room, where pianists play in winter (including Montreux jazz artist Al Copley, a long-term guest and friend of Suzane's). Bedrooms have pale walls and parquet, down-filled duvets on plain pine beds, perhaps a balcony or a chaise longue. All have views that sweep down across the little village to the majestic Eiger. There's a big garden for summer, too. Charming, rustic Wengen is known as 'the birthplace of alpine skiing'; the Falken is one of its oldest hotels.

rooms	50: 48 twins/doubles, 2 suites.
price	Chf180-Chf330.
meals	Dinner Chf30; book ahead
closed	Mid-April-mid-May; mid-October-mid-December.
directions	Park at Lauterbrunnen & take train to Wengen. Call ahead to arrange pick up from station.

Hotel

piste or lift	50m	Suzane Cova-Seliciano
lift for bikes	100m	tel +41 (0)33 856 5121
village centre	100m	fax +41 (0)33 855 3339
		e-mail info@hotelfalken.com
		web www.hotelfalken.com

Map 6   Entry 87

Romantik Hotel Schweizerhof
3818 Grindelwald, Switzerland

It was one of the first hotels to be built in traditional Grindelwald – darkly, splendidly wooden with a hundred red shutters and geraniums to match. A few changes have been introduced since 1892 – not least indoor pool, spa, bowling alley and gym – but you still get all the carved wood, open fires and wingback chairs you could desire. Staff (delightful to a fault) wear regional Swiss dress, food, accompanied by music from the zither, has an international flavour, in keeping with the crowd who come here – and come back, year after year. Bedrooms are big and impeccably Swiss, furnished with antiques and flowers; velvety red-curtained French windows open to small private balconies that overlook the soaring Eiger and Wetterhorn. At the entrance is a fancy retro-cab that takes you to and from the train station – a traditional touch in keeping with the feel of both hotel and resort. If for nothing else come for the Jungfraujoch, the highest railway station in Europe.

rooms	50: 34 twins/doubles, 16 suites.
price	Half-board Chf235-Chf445.
meals	Half-board only.
closed	Easter-May; 5 October-20 December.
directions	From Grindelwald, left at train station. Hotel 200m on right.

Hotel

	Anneliese & Otto Hauser-Seger	
tel	+41 (0)33 853 2202	
fax	+41 (0)33 853 2004	
e-mail	info@hotel-schweizerhof.com	
web	www.hotel-schweizerhof.com	

piste or lift	500m
cross-country trail	500m
lift for bikes	500m
village centre	50m

Map 6   Entry 88

Chalet-Hotel Gletschergarten
3818 Grindelwald, Switzerland

Bursting with red and pink window boxes in summer, the grand old hotel sits on the edge of the town, a mini trot up the hill. Grindelwald has a long-standing relationship with the winter-sporting Brits, and the Breitensteins have a soft spot for English-speaking guests. The place is magnificent with panelled ceilings and old family pieces, Grandpa's paintings and roses from the garden; the sitting room, with its stag's head on the chimney breast, rugs and deep armchairs, has a Scottish lodge feel. The dining room has a picture window to pull in the views; and you breakfast in the stübe, where little alcoves hold religious antique carvings, the ceramic stove has a built-in seat-warmer and a cushioned bench skirts dark panelled walls. Bedrooms, by contrast, are smartly modern, with furniture in light pine; teddy bears and heart-shaped chocolates dress the pillows. Every room has a balcony, and the corner rooms have the best views. A deeply comfortable chalet hotel, walking distance from the handsome village yet away from the tourist throng. *Minimum stay three nights.*

rooms	26: 19 twins/doubles, 7 triples.
price	Chf210-Chf260.
	Singles Chf110-Chf150.
meals	Dinner Chf38-Chf45.
closed	April-mid-May;
	mid-October-mid-December.
directions	Hotel 300m from village centre, on left.

Hotel

piste or lift	500m	
cross-country trail	500m	
lift for bikes	500m	
village centre	300m	

		Elsbeth & Finn Breitenstein
tel		+41 (0)33 853 1721
fax		+41 (0)33 853 2957
e-mail		gletschergarten@grindelwald.ch
web		www.hotel-gletschergarten.ch

Map 6 Entry 89

Hotel Garbo
Rue de Medran 5, 1936 Verbier, Switzerland

After a tough day on the slopes this is the place to come home to – within stumbling distance of the clubs and bars that make Verbier's nightlife so dashing. Behind a red-shuttered exterior Daniel has created a smart, new reception area (white-tiled floor, black designer chairs); to the right is the restaurant, woodily traditional yet chic, with long tables and log fire. If the hearty platters of French food are not your style, there's a second restaurant that deals in Japanese noodles and (takeaway) sushi. Bedrooms are simple, modern, comfortable, with more Japanese touches: white walls, paper lampshades, a pine bed and a balcony (though not every room has one). But with Murphy's Bar downstairs you'll be spending little time up here. Square barstools, sharp lines, strong drinks, a lively crowd – get the night off to a flying start. Just about everything starts at the Garbo's door: shops, restaurants, clubs, cafés, bars, trails... and lifts to some of the most fearsome pistes in the world.

rooms	25: 23 twins/doubles, 1 quadruple, 1 family room for 5.
price	Chf140-Chf250.
meals	Dinner Chf40-Chf80.
closed	May-mid-July; September-mid-November.
directions	In centre of Verbier. Bear right after tourist office. Hotel 150m on left.

Hotel

	Daniel Vonwyss	piste or lift	100m
tel	+41 (0)27 771 6272	cross-country trail	2km
fax	+41 (0)27 771 6271	lift for bikes	100m
e-mail	info@hotelgarbo.com	village centre	10m
web	www.hotelgarbo.com		

Map 6   Entry 90

Hotel Silvana
Furri, 3920 Zermatt, Switzerland

An electric-taxi ride up from Zermatt (or one stage on the gondola) brings you to the Silvana; sledges in winter whizz you down. This is our favourite sort of family hotel, charming and laid-back; you are surrounded by pastures in summer, pistes in winter, and the magnificent Tobleroned Matterhorn all year round. Dany and Felicitas give you five-course dinners in the restaurant (and a children's menu), local dishes in the dark-pine stübe, a sunny terrace and slopey, parasoled garden for summer, and a games room with a pool table for the children. Bedrooms are fresh and appealing, with pale carpets, modern pine, excellent mattresses, soft duvets, good bathrooms; a couple have a mezzanine under the eaves for extra beds. Your friendly hosts are fully hands on, and will organise your entire holiday if you let them: guided walks and bike rides, barbecues in the forest, sledging down to old cobbled Zermatt. Return to the hotel's wellness centre and be pampered by sauna, steam, jacuzzi and pool.

rooms	21 twins/doubles.
price	Half-board Chf110-Chf165.
meals	Half-board only.
closed	May-mid-June; November-October.
directions	A car-free resort. Park at Täsch & take shuttle train to Zermatt, then electric taxi to Klein Matterhorn Gondala (08.30-17.00). Hotel at 1st stage.

Hotel

piste or lift	100m		Dany & Felicitas Biner
cross-country trail	200m	tel	+41 (0)27 966 2800
lift for bikes	100m	fax	+41 (0)27 966 2805
village centre	4km	e-mail	silvana@zermatt.ch
		web	www.zermatt.ch/silvana

Map 6 Entry 91

Hotel Sonne
Postfach 121, 3920 Zermatt, Switzerland

Zermatt is the Belgravia of the Alps and here is a hotel to match. Up one of the narrow cobbled streets is the Sonne, its pebbled sun beaming up at you from the pavement outside. The family built the hotel 30 years ago, and keep it immaculately. In spite of swish and beautifully upholstered reproduction Louis XV chairs and state-of-the-art chandeliers, the atmosphere at the Sonne is relaxed and friendly. Abstract black and white photographs line the walls, and a modern glass walkway links the main building to an older chalet (and three more bedrooms) behind. In the pretty, panelled dining room you're treated to delicious Italian antipasti for dinner and homemade muesli at breakfast. Bedrooms are as good as you'd expect – walls fabric-clad, carpets deep blue, wood with a walnut veneer, duvets plumply white. Logs crackle contentedly in the vast stone fireplace in winter. And the wellness centre, whose sparkling white walls are decorated with palm murals, has everything – steam, sauna, whirlpool, massage and facials. Come and be spoiled.

rooms	45: 9 twins, 36 suites.
price	Chf276-Chf490.
	Suites Chf320-Chf620.
meals	Dinner Chf35-Chf65.
closed	Never.
directions	A car-free resort. Park at Täsch & take shuttle train to Zermatt, then electric taxi to hotel. Hotel on high street, 250m from station.

Hotel

	Fam. Forster-Lingg	piste or lift	300m
tel	+41 (0)27 966 2066	cross-country trail	300m
fax	+41 (0)27 966 2065	lift for bikes	300m
e-mail	sonne.zermatt@reconline.ch	village centre	50m
web	www.sonne.masch.com		

Map 6 Entry 92

Chalet Huwi
Wichjeweg, 3920 Zermatt, Switzerland

Lap up the sun on your south-facing balcony. The view is immaculate: a white octagonal chapel, the glittering Matterhorn behind. Huwi was once a family home, now it's a luxurious chalet. It's new but charming with a rustic feel, encircled by a garden and old mazots; hone your barbecue skills out here in summer. Inside, a harmonious mix of furniture – brightly-cushioned sofas, a grandfather clock, old country chests, a new pine table. Logs smoulder in the fire, fresh white walls are hung with prints and pictures, thick cotton curtains frame the French windows to the balcony. Kitchen and dining room are open plan; a British chalet girl cooks and cares for skiing guests. Bedrooms are on this floor and under the eaves, named after mountain flowers; Edelweiss, the biggest, with a balcony, is serenely all-white. All are simply furnished and very comfortable. In luscious Zermatt backpackers mingle with the bejewelled, horse-drawn carriages transport you to the shops, cable cars ferry you to 38 fine restaurants on the slopes.

rooms	Chalet for 8: 4 twins/doubles.
price	Chf5,900-Chf10,500 per week. Winter: Chf14,900 per week.
meals	Self-catering. Catered in winter.
closed	Never.
directions	Trains to Zermatt from Brig. Electric taxi from station to chalet.

Self-catering/Catered

piste or lift	600m	
cross-country trail	500m	
lift for bikes	600m	
village centre	800m	

Zermatt Holidays
tel +41 (0)27 968 1130
fax +41 (0)27 968 1132
e-mail zermattholidays@rhone.ch
web www.zermattholidays.com

Map 6 Entry 93

Waldhotel Fletschhorn
3906 Saas Fee, Switzerland

The Fletschhorn's delightful new owners are continuing the tradition of relaxed Swiss hospitality - and delicious food. Six-course dinners from head chef Markus Neff are matched by fine local wines from cellar-meister Charlie Neumüller, enjoyed on sunny days on the lovely cobbled dining terrace under a vine-clambered arbour. The setting is secluded and stunning, the building surrounded by forest. When we visited, the striking 60s façade was softened by sprigs of Christmas larch attached to the carved balconies - beautiful. In winter you feast in the stübe, soberly cosy in its dark wooden garb. But that's where the old days end: every other space in this small luxury hotel is a shrine to modernity. Upstairs, round windows lighten airy, unconventionally shaped rooms and all feels generous: big rugs, big beds, splashy art. There are steam bath and jacuzzi, and sculptures and paintings everywhere, some of it exhibited along a spot-lit corridor. The skiing is high, Saas Fee has some of the finest in Europe, and the hotel bus transports you to the slopes. *Two-day cookery courses available.*

rooms	14: 9 twins/doubles, 2 singles, 3 suites.	
price	Chf300. Singles Chf200. Suites Chf400-Chf500.	
meals	Dinner Chf145-Chf190.	
closed	May-mid-June; November-mid-December.	
directions	Park in main car park of this car-free village. Call hotel from freephone board to arrange taxi pick-up.	
Hotel		

	Charlie Neumüller & Markus Neff		piste or lift	2km
tel	+41 (0)27 957 2131		cross-country trail	2km
fax	+41 (0)27 957 2187		lift for bikes	2km
e-mail	info@fletschhorn.ch		village centre	2km
web	www.fletschhorn.ch			

Map 6   Entry 94

Hotel Fidazerhof
Via da Fidaz 34, Fidaz, 7019 Flims, Switzerland

It's the largest building in the hamlet, high above the village of Flims. The steep roof and intricately carved 1909 wooden façade stand in modest contrast to the sweeping ground floor with new-decked, south-facing terrace. Step into a fresh and contemporary, 10-room hotel that really does have your well-being at heart: the whole mood is one of thoughtful eco-consciousness. Come for shiatsu and Ayurvedic therapies (a huge range), and authentic regional food that flows from the kitchens. Both the interior and the exterior are white and woody, spotless and serene. Light pours into the restaurant, infused with the irresistible aromas of cheese and wine, sizzling meats (naturally reared, of course) and fragrant sauces; bedrooms are reached via the original wrought-iron stair. All are light and airy with white walls, polished wooden floors and modern textiles; suites have an arched doorway leading to a sitting area with a deep sofa; bathrooms are gorgeous. Antonia and Roland and their team have created a place of civilisation and rest – and there's a shuttle bus to take you to the slopes.

rooms	10: 5 twins/doubles, 5 suites.
price	Chf110-Chf200. Suites Chf180-Chf280.
meals	Dinner Chf45.
closed	Never.
directions	A13 Zurich-Chur; 10km to Reichenau; off main road, for Flims; hotel signed, 1km above Flims.

Hotel

piste or lift	2km		Antonia Schaerli & Roland Haefliger
cross-country trail	2km	tel	+41 (0)81 911 3503
lift for bikes	2km	fax	+41 (0)81 911 2175
village centre	2km	e-mail	info@fidazerhof.ch
		web	www.fidazerhof-flims.ch

Map 1 Entry 95

Chesa Grischuna
Bahnhofstrasse 12, 7250 Klosters, Switzerland

It is the alpine hotel to which the rest aspire. The days when Cary Grant and Gene Kelly came linger in the memory; now the Grischuna is more beautiful than ever. Many guests return year on year – for the Guler family and their staff, as attentive as the day (all those days ago, in 1938) they opened their doors, and for an atmosphere as warm. The restaurant is heaven, Swiss-style – aged timbers, carved columns, crisp curtains, fresh flowers, an old ski hitched to a chunky beam. It's popular, of course; at winter lunchtimes the worn tiled floors are scattered with chunks of snow as skiers stomp in and cheery waiters ferry piping hot plates of delicious food to the table; a young chef delivers modern dishes with an Italian edge. Upstairs – and in the *chalet de charme* over the way – creaky stairs lead to pale-panelled bedrooms, each individual in shape and design. A small bar with frescoed walls of winter scenes and a full-size bowling alley share the vaulted basement. Swim, skate, ski, curl: you are bang in the middle of old Klosters, cherished haunt of Prince Charles.

rooms	Chesa for 14: 9 doubles, 5 singles. Chalet for 9: 7 doubles, 2 singles.
price	Chf220–Chf460. Chalet Chf180–Chf350.
meals	Dinner Chf45.
closed	May–June; mid–October–mid–December.
directions	In centre of Klosters.

Hotel

	Fam. Guler		
tel	+41 (0)81 422 2222	piste or lift	50m
fax	+41 (0)81 422 2225	cross-country trail	300m
e-mail	chesagrischuna@bluewin.ch	lift for bikes	50m
web	www.chesagrischuna.ch	village centre	10m

Map 2 Entry 96

ArtHausHotel
Platzstrasse 5, 7270 Davos Platz, Switzerland

Davos may be no great shakes in the 'character' stakes, but do you get chic boutiques, mountain trains and the romance of the horse-drawn sleigh. Diego Clavadetscher has painted the walls of his townhouse hotel a deep red with grand detail around the windows. A patron of the arts he often holds exhibitions here, so local work dots the pine-knotted walls. In the sunny, informal dining room a trolley bar brims with unusual varieties of schnapps and a score of whisky malts, some of the liquor finding its way into the tasty dishes. Meaty stew *pizokels* is one speciality, fish is big too. There's also a smaller restaurant, smart with a grand piano (sadly, too ancient to play). Bedrooms differ; many have fine pine-panelled ceilings and small sitting area, all are large and light; furniture is basic pine, curtains are blue, bathrooms shine whitely. For history and architecture get the bus to Davos Dorf; for explosive nightlife – starting somewhere around late afternoon – step outside the door. Diego is the kindest of hosts.

rooms	19 twins/doubles.
price	Chf148-Chf258.
meals	Dinner Chf45-Chf95.
	Half-board option: extra Chf25 p.p.
closed	May-November.
directions	1st right after tourist office in Davos Platz. Hotel on left.

Hotel

piste or lift	300m		Diego Clavadetscher
cross-country trail	500m	tel	+41 (0)81 413 5104
lift for bikes	300m	fax	+41 (0)81 413 7773
village centre	50m	e-mail	arthaushotel@arthaushotel.ch
		web	www.arthaushotel.ch

Map 2 Entry 97

Chalet-Hotel Larix
Obere Albertistrasse 9, 7270 Davos Platz, Switzerland

One of the prettiest chalets in Davos – and the only chalet-hotel. John's family built the Larix in 1953 as their home and the fine furniture has been passed down, along with the family spirit. Hospitality runs in the blood: son David (Scottish-born, Davos-reared) runs another inn with a Michelin star. The Larix has two dining rooms – one that sparkles at night and serves modern French dishes, the other a woody stübe; both are worth seeking out. Off reception is an intimate, panelled sitting room with comfortable leather chairs, magazines, books and greenery. Ask for one of the bedrooms in the house rather than the annexe: refreshingly individual in shape and character, they have white walls, aqua carpets, modern art, simple good taste. Some have pine cladding, others are under the eaves, all are a good size. You are a two-minute walk from the shuttle that takes you to the trains (gateway to some glorious hiking and skiing) and seven minutes from the slopes. There's a super wellness centre, too – and a wagging Saint Bernard.

rooms	21: 14 twins/doubles, 5 triples, 1 family rooms, 1 suite.
price	Chf140-Chf320.
meals	Half-board option: extra Chf30 p.p.
closed	May-June & November.
directions	Through Davos Platz towards Frauenkirch; right at end of village, by bus station Alberti; signed.

Hotel

	John & Rita Henderson	piste or lift	1km
tel	+41 (0)81 413 1188	cross-country trail	900m
fax	+41 (0)81 413 3349	lift for bikes	1km
e-mail	hotel-larix@bluewin.ch	village centre	1.5km
web	www.hotel-larix.ch		

Map 1 Entry 98

Arlenwald Hotel
Restaurant Burestübli, 7050 Arosa, Switzerland

The young British staff keep him on his toes; Heinrich – "call me Henry" – has a sense of humour and enjoys the latest slang. He's owned and run this restaurant with rooms for 10 years – you can ski from the door. The snow falls deeply here, high above Arosa – it's a slippery drive in winter, but an exhilarating one. Scrunch your way to the front door and be ushered into the kitchen, where Tyrolean yodelling soars from a modern plasma screen – a typical touch. This hotel may be steeped in character but it is stylishly kitted out. The restaurant itself is warm and inviting with its mix of Swiss country antiques, knotted pine, carved pillars, green-tiled stove – always a buzz. Big windows open to forest; bird tables attract wildlife as you wolf down delicious regional dishes – or feast on homemade jams. The small sitting room has a fish tank, plants, internet access and books. Bedrooms, some cosily under the eaves, are beamed, duvets are fashionably striped, shower rooms ultra new. After a day's piste-bashing, come home to herb-infused steam in the stunning sauna-with-a-view.

rooms	8: 4 twins/doubles, 2 singles, 2 suites.
price	Chf200-Chf300.
meals	Dinner Chf30.
closed	May-June.
directions	From Chur to Arosa; right opposite Esso garage for 3km to end of road. Ask for Restaurant Burstubli; hotel in same building.

Hotel

piste or lift	10m		Heinrich Schwendener
cross-country trail	50m	tel	+41 (0)81 377 1838
lift for bikes	2km	fax	+41 (0)81 377 4550
village centre	2km	e-mail	arlenwald@bluewin.ch
		web	www.arlenwaldhotel.ch

Map 1   Entry 99

Chesa Salis
7502 Bever, Switzerland

The noble von Salis family built the villa in 1590 on the pastured fringe of the village. And it's very special inside, elegantly rustic, its warm yellow walls hung with colourful oils – Jurg and Sibylla, who've been here two years, put on exhibitions of local art. Carefully restored examples of traditional craftsmanship are everywhere, along with choice family pieces, dressers, chests, even the odd agricultural antique. A small dining room/library leads off the reception, and there's a larger restaurant at the back delivering classic Italian and French dishes whose ingredients are flown in daily from around the world (this is St Moritz territory, after all!). There's also a smaller restaurant specialising in grills: Jurg himself roasts the meats in front of you. Each of the bedrooms is different: some grand with chandeliers and painted ceilings, others pine-clad, all carpeted and comfortable. Expect low ceilings and doorways in the rooms in the oldest part of the house; those in the attic ooze history and charm. The Engadine spreads its beauty before you, and the Degiacomis are delightful.

rooms	17 twins/doubles.
price	Chf185-Chf330.
meals	Dinner Chf54.
closed	April-May; November.
directions	From St Moritz, follow signs to Celerina & on to Bever; left. Hotel on left.

Hotel

	Jurg & Sibylla Degiacomi	piste or lift	4km
tel	+41 (0)81 851 1616	cross-country trail	10m
fax	+41 (0)81 851 1600	lift for bikes	4km
e-mail	reception@chesa-salis.ch	village centre	50m
web	www.chesa-salis.ch		

Map 2 Entry 100

Chesa Rosatsch
7505 Celerina-St Moritz, Switzerland

Few places have a better setting, a more absorbing history or a more delightful staff. Over the years the Chesa has been transformed from four fascinating buildings into one super hotel, linked by a glass-roofed restaurant. Young Ueli Knobel has introduced contemporary touches to the bar: a geometric carpet, a zinc counter, a hundred whiskies, a humidor crammed with rare cigars. Decorations change with the seasons, as do the dishes on the menu. Stübe and restaurant are a delight, with 300-year-old panelled walls and ceilings, and crisp-clothed tables sparkling with glass. Slopey corridors upstairs reflect the building's age. Bedrooms are not in keeping with the old Engadine feel, but are no less comforting for that. All are carpeted and have pale-painted wardrobes and flowery drapes; some are under the white eaves; pristine-walled bathrooms have fine granite basins. The suite, woodily traditonal, comes with river views. Modest Celerina is at the door, its stone houses embellished with traditional *graffito*, and you get a private shuttle to transport you to the lifts. Splendid.

rooms	35: 34 twins/doubles, 1 suite.
price	€170–€410; suite €390–€650.
meals	Dinner from €45.
closed	Mid-April-mid-June.
directions	From St Moritz, signs to Celerina. Third exit off roundabout; right past Co-op. Hotel 150m on left.

Hotel

piste or lift	3km
cross-country trail	500m
lift for bikes	3km
village centre	200m

Ueli Knobel

tel	+41 (0)81 837 0101
fax	+41 (0)81 837 0100
e-mail	hotel@rosatsch.ch
web	www.rosatsch.ch

Map 2 Entry 101

Hotel Misani
7505 St Moritz-Celerina, Switzerland

A slice of the city close to glamorous St Moritz. The Misani is full of surprises – smiling faces and off-beat ideas behind a classic façade. Smooth leather armchairs pull up to glass-topped tables before a streamlined fire, spots embedded in floors illuminate modern art. But it's not all "designer decadence", to coin Jürg's phrase. Ethnicity comes from pieces collected on travels, and the stübe is deliciously old (its caramel panelling treated once a month to a special milk wash). Bedrooms vary in size, most are superb, and several are extravagantly themed and very groovy – try Arabian Nights, Savannah Sunsets or Deep Ocean Sleep. Original thinking extends to children's colouring pens at dinner and the customising of rooms: choose from electronic wizardry, books, games, antlers, throws... or even a songbird in a cage. Breakfasts can be coffee with brioche or caviar and champagne; dinners are market-fresh with an irreverent twist. Keep up with the blue bloods in town – hurtling down the Cresta by day, hitting the Bollinger by night. *Minimum stay in apartments one week.*

rooms	35 + 3: 29 doubles, 4 singles, 1 suite, 1 family suite. 3 apartments for 2-4 with kitchenettes.
price	Chf150-Chf330. Singles Chf135-Chf165. Suites Chf460-Chf620. Apartments Chf180-Chf420.
meals	Dinner Chf50-Chf120.
closed	April-June; mid-October-November.
directions	From St Moritz, signs to Celerina; left at r'bout; on left.
Hotel	

	Jürg Mettler
tel	+41 (0)81 833 3314
fax	+41 (0)81 833 0937
e-mail	info@hotelmisani.ch
web	www.hotelmisani.ch

piste or lift	500m
cross-country trail	500m
lift for bikes	500m
village centre	10m

Map 2 Entry 102

Photography by Nick Woodford

italy

Chalet Faure
Albergo e Centro Benessere, Via Chaberton 4, 10050 Sauze d'Oulx, Italy

Sprawling Sauze d'Oulx (pronounced Sow-zee-doo) mushroomed in the 1970s, thanks to the Milky Way ski circuit that links with French Montgenevre. The small hotel, reconstructed from an 1890 chalet, hides down a narrow, paved street lined with cafés, boutiques and bars. On the first floor find a modern, Italian-style reception: wooden floors, shiny leather sofas, halogen lights sparkling onto old bricks, an oriental rug. The bar, with its exposed beams, stone floor and open log fire, has a warm and friendly mood – a little refuge from the lively, young-Brit-friendly village. Bedrooms are up a floor, half under the eaves, the rest with old beams; some have a mezzanine (fun for kids), others a balcony overlooking the village; all have framed black and white pictures on the walls, and glossy bedcovers with bathrooms to match. In the beauty centre: herbal and steam baths, a masseuse and a range of treatments, some of which are free to summer guests. You also get your own ski hire shop and on-the-spot ski instructor, Frederico.

rooms	11: 6 doubles, 4 triples, 1 quadruple.
price	€120–€150.
meals	Set menu in nearby restaurant, €15–€20.
closed	Mid-April-mid-June; October-November.
directions	Off Via Assietta in village centre.

Hotel

piste or lift	300m		Frederico Faure
cross-country trail	1.5km	tel	+39 0122 859760
lift for bikes	300m	fax	+39 0122 853928
village centre	10m	e-mail	chaletfaure@libero.it
		web	www.chaletfaure.it

Map 5 Entry 103

La Barme
Valnontey, 11012 Cogne, Italy

Rest your head in an 18th-century mountain dairy in the Grand Paradis National Park. Old stone foundations support weathered beams, split by the high altitude sun; small shuttered windows peep out from the lauze-stone roof. Inside, a cosy pine-clad living room with a wood-burning stove, light modern tiles warmed by colourful rag rugs, rustic tables and chairs and soft lights. In the dining room wine bottles line the shelves, old agricultural tools hang from the walls, aromas of local dishes waft through from the kitchen. Given the old feel of the place, the bedrooms have surprisingly modern furniture with built-in beds and wardrobes – but there's no shortage of character, with beamy ceilings stuffed under the eaves and bright curtains at little windows. In summer, little Valnontey may bustle, but the rest of the year there's splendid seclusion. Swiss-born Andrea and Stefano are lovely and can tell you everything you need to know; come for hiking, biking and trekking, cross-country skiing, sleigh rides to the old village of Valmiana, and ice-climbing, a rare thrill. The action starts in nearby Cogne.

rooms	15: 8 twins/doubles, 7 triples.
price	Half-board €45–€60 p.p.
meals	Half-board only. Picnic lunch €6.
closed	October-November.
directions	Exit A5 Aosta Ovest for Cogne for 21km. Over roundabout for village centre for 100m; right for Valnontey for 3km. Hotel 1st on left on entering hamlet.

Hotel

	Andrea & Stefano di Herren
tel	+39 0165 749177
fax	+39 0165 749213
e-mail	labarme@tiscalinet.it
web	www.hotellabarme.com

piste or lift	2.5km
cross-country trail	50m
lift for bikes	2.5km
village centre	2.5km

Map 6 Entry 104

Hotel Petit Giles
Villaggio Gimillan 118, 11012 Cogne, Italy

High on south-facing slopes above the pretty village of Cogne is a hamlet blessed with sensational views. The church dates from 1600 and the dwellings that surround it are not much younger. In saving this one from ruin, the Gimillan family have created a quietly authentic place to stay. From outside the place looks small – a jumble of heavy stone roofs and simple wooden balconies – but inside all is light, bright and roomy. You get a roaring fire in the large, lively, public bar, and cosy bedrooms under the eaves. Table lamps, dried flowers, pretty patterned bedspreads and country antiques, pure white walls, dark carpets, new rafters and an undeniably feminine feel. Bathrooms are brand new, and every room has one. Outside are two big sunny terraces lined with deckchairs, and because of the position you get six hours of sunshine even on the shortest (clear!) day. In June the Valle de Grozon bursts into colour and botanists from around the world come together to discover some of the rarest specimans in the Alps; in winter the area is known for its cross-country trails.

rooms	11: 4 doubles, 5 twins, 2 triples.
price	€52–€66.
meals	Bar snacks. Restaurant 100m.
closed	May & November-December.
directions	Exit A5 Aosta Ovest for Cogne for 21km. Left at roundabout for Gimillan for 4km. Hotel in village centre, at end of road.

Hotel

piste or lift	2.5km	
cross-country trail	2.5km	
lift for bikes	2.5km	
village centre	2.5km	

	Fam. Gimillan
tel	+39 0165 74363
fax	+39 0165 74272
e-mail	info@petitgiles.com
web	www.petitgiles.com

Map 6 Entry 105

Hotel Bellevue
Rue Grand Paradis 22, 11012 Cogne, Italy

Hotel Bellevue is a blessed mix of exclusive and understated. It is also the sole hotel in the valley, nudging the fringes of this ancient village of cobbled streets and craft shops. And its décor is as breathtaking as its views. One of the treatment rooms is an alpage chalet with a copper Cleopatra tub, the lift has been created from an old confessional – Signora Jeantet-Roullet's imagination is as boundless as her husband's interpretative skills are impressive. Beautiful old wood, antique furniture, fine pictures… each room a surprise. The children's playroom comes with a blackboard, old school desks and wooden hobby horse, some of the suites have real fires, others rustic four-posters. The restaurant is renowned and much of the food homegrown in summer – there's a circular potager in the grounds. There are also plenty of private corners in which to worship the sun, on a mahogany lounger under an Egyptian cotton parasol. The happy Jeantet-Roullet family has created one of the most gorgeous hotels in the Alps: an inspiration and a joy.

rooms	38 + 3: 31 twins/doubles, 7 suites for 3. 3 chalets for 2-6.
price	€140-€286. Singles €110-€220. Suites €285-€396. Chalets €280-€352.
meals	Dinner €38-€58.
closed	October-December.
directions	Exit A5 Aosta Ovest for Cogne for 21km. Over roundabout for village centre for 100m; right for Valnontey. Hotel 100m on right.
Hotel	

	Fam. Jeantet-Roullet
tel	+39 0165 74825
fax	+39 0165 749192
e-mail	info@hotelbellevue.it
web	www.hotelbellevue.it

piste or lift	200m
cross-country trail	10m
lift for bikes	200m
village centre	50m

Map 6 Entry 106

Notre Maison
Fraz Cretaz, 11012 Cogne, Italy

If you love the good life, you'll love it here. Herbs and vegetables come from the potager, the cellar vaults 160 bins. And it's a peaceful spot, a mile from the village centre. The building is 20 years old, of a modern design that blends well with the surroundings. Vast timbers in the entrance sweep up to the eaves to support the stone lauzes that make up the roof; windows are large and open onto a super garden, with areas for wild flowers and a small botanical bed. Doze off on loungers dotted among the neatly-cut hills of grass, then cool off in the spa's pool and swim against the current. The living room has a massive, ultra-modern open fireplace right in its middle. The bigger bedrooms, too, have open fires, and space for a smart sofa or two. Rafters are sloped, drapes are generous, walls are turquoise, pink or moss green. 'Superior' rooms have baths as well as showers. You breakfast off white china on red-clothed tables, there's a well-being centre for grown-ups, a video cartoon room for the kids and mountain bikes for all.
An excellent, family-friendly hotel, in cross-country ski heaven.

rooms	23: 21 twins/doubles, 2 suites for 4.
price	€70–€180. Half-board €58–€110 p.p.
meals	Dinner €25–€30.
closed	May–June; October–December.
directions	Exit A5 Aosta Ovest for Cogne for 20km to Cretaz. Hotel 100m on left.

Hotel

piste or lift	2km	
cross–country trail	50m	
lift for bikes	1.5km	
village centre	2km	

		Sig. Celesia
tel		+39 0165 74104
fax		+39 0165 749186
e–mail		hotel@notremaison.it
web		www.notremaison.it

Map 6 Entry 107

Lo Ratelë

Fraz. Ville 33, 11010 Allein, Italy

Paola is a true countrywoman, with twinkling eyes and feet planted firmly on the ground. Her cooking and the views are two good reasons for coming here; and the bistro, simply converted from old, arched animal stalls, is popular with all. Hams, sausages, country soups and home-baked black bread are specialities, as is *la coppa del'amicizia* – a hot coffee and liqueur drink slurped with friends from a multi-spouted wooden bowl. Meat – goat, veal, lamb – is home-reared on the small family farm; vegetables come fresh from Paola's patch. The old-fashioned kitchen is packed with gleaming jars of home-produced goodies so ask in your best French or Italian (Paola speaks no English) if you can buy some to take home. Bedrooms are basic but spotless and it's a joy to have one at the front. Stand on your balcony and be wowed by the view that sweeps across the wide, lush valley to the snow-capped mountains beyond. Lo Ratelë's long, traditional stone front is scarlet with geraniums in summer.

rooms	7 doubles.
price	Half-board €39–€44 p.p.
meals	Half-board only.
closed	January–April.
directions	From Aosta, route 27. After Gignod right for Allein on A2, signed.

Bed & Breakfast

	Paola Conchâtre
tel	+39 0165 78265
fax	+39 0165 78265

piste or lift	9km
cross–country trail	9km
lift for bikes	9km
village centre	250m

Map 6 Entry 108

Chalet Alpina
11016 La Thuile, Italy

Edy is from Johannesburg and met Nicole skiing in Chamonix. After a visit to La
Thuile (ex mining village: not the prettiest place) they decided to open a
guesthouse, and launched the pretty Chalet Alpina. The renovations continue.
The low, warm-yellow chalet is shaded by a weeping willow at the back, while the
entrance is guarded by a pair of old wooden skis. Up the granite stairs to
bedrooms (mostly) under the eaves. Functional, with built-in wardrobes and dark-
stained tables and chairs, they have floral bedspreads and curtains match, net at
the windows and hardwearing carpeting on the floors. In the pine-clad lounge:
a new open fire in one corner and Ikea-style furniture and 1970s leather sofas.
There's a well-stocked bar with some South African labels; on the other side are
tables and chairs neatly arranged around a long table in anticipation of breakfast.
Dinner (half-board option) is at a nearby restaurant. Your kind hosts are ski
instructors and you couldn't be closer to the lift… in summer you have tennis and
an outdoor pool. It's friendly, young and fun.

rooms	14: 10 twins/doubles, 3 singles, 1 triple.
price	€60–€110. Singles €45–€80. Half-board €45–€70 p.p.
meals	Half-board at restaurant nearby.
closed	May & October-November. Call to check.
directions	Exit A5 Morgex-Courmayeur; at Pré St Didier, left to La Thuile; through village; first left; on right.

Bed & Breakfast

piste or lift	300m		Edy & Nicole Nico
cross-country trail	400m	tel	+39 0165 884187
lift for bikes	400m	e-mail	chaletalpina@lathuile.it
village centre	500m	web	www.chaletalpina.it

Map 5 Entry 109

Hotel Dolonne
Dolonne, 11013 Courmayeur, Italy

The stone walls are more than a metre thick in some places and you can see where the building was hewn out of the rock. The 16th-century fort once protected the livestock and inhabitants of tiny Dolonne; later it was partly burnt down in the Napoleonic Wars; today it is a family-run hotel with a luxurious feel. New balconies run up the grey-stone front, bright with geraniums in summer. Lounges are comfortable with antiques and open fires; lights have been ingeniously crafted from old fruit presses; the dining room is candlelit. Many of the bedrooms are under the eaves with an extra bed on the mezzanine. They are serenely furnished with rustic wardrobes and chests of drawers, rich bedspreads, floor-to-ceiling curtains, polished floors. Barbara was once a pharmacist — hence the scales, dusty old books and jars of potions that embellish the place; she is also an enthusiastic consumer of herbal teas and the hotel has quite a collection. You are yards from the ski lift in winter, and a short walk from the centre of classy Courmayeur. For summer, a golf course and a fishing reserve await.

rooms	26: 20 twins/doubles, 6 triples.
price	€70–€160.
meals	Dinner €20–€45.
closed	Rarely.
directions	From Courmayeur, follow signs to Dolonne. Hotel in Dolonne centre.

Hotel

	Barbara & Edy Vaglio Tessitore
tel	+39 0165 846674
fax	+39 0165 846671
e-mail	hoteldolonne@hoteldolonne.it
web	www.hoteldolonne.com

piste or lift	150m
cross-country trail	150m
lift for bikes	1.5km
village centre	800m

Map 5 Entry 110

Laurent Meuble
Via Circonvallazione 23, 11013 Courmayeur, Italy

In the middle of chic, cobbled Courmayeur, a modest bolthole. The old farmhouse became an inn in 1968, when the ski resort was beginning to buzz, and has been in the family ever since. (Signor Berthod slips off to New York in the holidays to brush up on his English.) A wooden balcony wraps its way around the front and sides of the pretty, whitewashed building; most bedrooms have their own little piece. Inside are a breakfast room with a small bar and comfortable sitting area, and a small, sunny *sala lettura* (reading room) furnished with Louis XVI-style sofa and fauteuils. Board games and houseplants add a comely touch. Bedrooms upstairs are larger than you might expect, and have polished wooden floors, pine cladding and pale walls. The furniture is nothing special, but soft lights, mirrors and fresh flowers give the rooms a lift. Coordinated fabrics are floral; old-fashioned bar radiators generate a good heat. There's no dining room, but who needs one when the gastronomic centre of the skiing world lies at your door?

rooms	14: 10 twins/doubles, 2 singles, 2 triples.
price	€ 70–€ 120.
meals	Restaurants nearby.
closed	Never.
directions	Exit A5 for Courmayeur. Keep right as road forks at Piazza del Monte Bianco. On left after 50m.

Bed & Breakfast

piste or lift	150m			Laurent Berthod
cross–country trail	50m	tel		+39 0165 846687
lift for bikes	150m	fax		+39 0165 844568
village centre	100m	e–mail		info@meublelaurent.com
		web		www.meublelaurent.com

Map 5   Entry 111

Pilier d'Angle
Via Grandes Jorasses 18, Entrèves , 11013 Courmayeur, Italy

Tiny, pretty Entrèves lies in the beautiful shadow of Mont Blanc. Pilier d'Angle was once a farmhouse; its pitched stone roof, dark timbers and whitewashed walls are typical of the region. Step into reception, the walls sporting a mix of rustic tools and framed black and white photographs of a 1970s restoration, then down to the Austrian-style stübe with its pine-clad walls, carved and cushioned wooden benches, country dresser lined with tin plates and open fire. Francesco, a true Italian, loves his food and treats you to four courses of regional delights. The larger restaurant, half a floor up, has skylight windows, so you can gaze in awe at Mont Blanc's peaks from your pretty, pink-clothed table. Four of the bedrooms have a mezzanine for an extra bed, most come with balconies, and the varnished wood is softened by cushions, houseplants and warm lighting. A second chalet has been built next door and has three apartments with kitchenettes and open fireplaces, perfect for families. Snow is guaranteed, thanks to an army of cannons; there's even more to do in summer.

rooms	18 + 3: 12 twins/doubles, 4 triples with mezzanine, 2 family rooms. 3 apartments for 4-6.
price	€84-€148. Half-board €54-€105 p.p.
meals	Lunch à la carte €30-€50.
closed	May & October-November.
directions	From France through Mont Blanc tunnel. Entrèves first village after tunnel; from village centre, 100m on left, signed.
Hotel	

	Francesco Pizzato	piste or lift	250m
tel	+39 0165 869760	cross-country trail	3km
fax	+39 0165 869770	lift for bikes	250m
e-mail	info@pilierdangle.it	village centre	2km
web	www.pilierdangle.it		

Map 5 Entry 112

Auberge de la Maison
Fraz. Entrèves, 11013 Courmayeur, Italy

Something quite special: a quietly elegant auberge with an exclusive yet unintimidating feel – thanks to friendly staff and a wagging dog. You're in the old part of the village of Val Fenet, enveloped by terraces, gardens and meadows, a couple of miles from cobbled Courmayeur. A strong Tuscan influence is detectable in the décor, not surprisingly: the owner is Florentine. His collection of promotional posters, oil paintings and prints of Val d'Aosta makes an impressive display on the walls, while a small reassembled mazot, complete with armchairs and reading lamps, is an interesting addition to the rug-strewn, woody reception. The lovely sitting room has logs stacked by the fire, the dining room is charming, and the bedrooms are mellow, uncluttered and stylish; spacious, too. Some have a third bed in the guise of a sofa, nearly all have a balcony, and views range from good to superb. And there's a small fitness centre, with a sauna and hydromassage. Fish for trout or play a round of golf in summer; in winter, ski right to the lift or don crampons for a snowy ascent. What a setting!

rooms	35: 29 doubles, 3 family rooms, 3 suites.
price	€ 105–€ 175. Suites € 175–€ 235.
meals	Dinner € 30.
closed	May.
directions	Exit A5 Traforo del Monte Bianco for Courmayeur & Entrèves. Down hill & 1st left, a narrow road signed Entrèves. Hotel on right.

Hotel

piste or lift	150m	
cross-country trail	1.5km	tel
lift for bikes	4km	fax
village centre	4km	e-mail
		web

Leo Garin
tel +39 0165 869811
fax +39 0165 869759
e-mail info@aubergemaison.it
web www.aubergemaison.it

Map 5 Entry 113

Petit Coin de Paradis
Loc. Vetan 19, 11010 Saint Pierre, Italy

Wide open meadows, marmots, chamois, wild flowers, views. At 1,680m above sea level, surrounded by high alp and snow-capped mountains, the setting is supreme. Undeniably a 'little corner of heaven' – and what was once a hamlet of ancient dwellings has become a vibrant B&B. (Or you can self-cater if you prefer.) The old stone houses have pretty wooden balconies tossed with flowers, lush lawns are dotted with summer toys. In winter, snowshoes, sledges, skis and bobsleighs are all for hire. The whole relaxed set-up bounces with bonhomie – thanks to friendly Daniela who has decorated from scratch to her own country designs. Walls are a mix of fresh whitewash and modern knotted pine; there are little tables and chairs and wood-burning stoves, bright ginghams, lacy lampshades, Swiss cottons. Some of the bedrooms are reached by ladder-like stairs. Just across the track is a tiny whitewashed church, silhouetted against the mountains and the sky; to the south lie the splendours of the Gran Paradiso National Park. All this, and nougat and *torcetti* for breakfast.

rooms	3 apartments: 1 for 2; 2 for 5.
price	€65. Singles €37.
meals	Agriturismo 50m up hill. Self-catering possible.
closed	Rarely.
directions	Exit A5 Aosta Ovest for Saint Pierre. Left at 1st set of lights; right to St Nicolas & on to Vetan for 8km.

Bed & Breakfast

	Daniela Berlier	piste or lift	1km
tel	+39 0165 908970	cross-country trail	10m
fax	+39 0165 908970	village centre	10m
e-mail	info@bebvetan.it		
web	www.bebvetan.it		

Map 6 Entry 114

Rifugio della Montagna
South Side, Big White Mountain, Italy

Such an unusual face has your host that he almost featured on the cover of the book. His lively, yet somewhat wooden, expression of surprise is a delight to those who meet him. And he lives in the strangest of places, far from the human race on the edge of a mountain on the side of a snow-filled valley. Only the most indomitable and foolhardy of you will venture that far, or take us on trust. But the skiing is at your door, the snow almost guaranteed, the silence tangible. Here the 'great white mantle has indeed girt the world', the razor-edge of the mountain ridge protecting you from other skiers. Years ago a party of mountain climbers disappeared here and the hut was built for a prolonged rescue operation. How mine host has the temerity to call such a basic, windowless hut a ski-lodge we dare not ask, for he has been known to cast interrogators from the mountain side. But our quest for peace and authenticity has led us here and we dare not retreat. We urge you to give it a go, for nothing will be gained from a fear of venturing.

rooms	1 double with open-air w.c.
price	Arbitrary.
meals	Well chilled.
closed	Never (no door).
directions	Follow yeti tracks; snow shoes, map, compass & crampons recommended.

piste or lift	0m		Signor Irato Yeti
cross-country trail	0m	tel	Messages by yodel only
village centre	150km		

Baita Layet
Zona Lago Blu, 11021 Cervinia, Italy

In winter, you and your bags are transported by 4x4. Baita Layet, built around a 14th-century chapel and still owned by the church, waits at the end of a rough, one-mile track – a haven above Cervinia's bustle. Friendly Luca Giani and his two daughters run the place, and renovated the building four years ago. An old stove warms the simple breakfast room where wooden farm implements decorate the walls, shimmering Klimt prints brighten the dark country furniture, rugs strew the floors. Bedrooms are big, modern and spotless, with new pine beds, a couple of chairs, rag rugs on gleaming floors, underfloor heating and soundproofed doors. It's bitter here in winter, so windows are doubled glazed and walls have extra insulation. The views to the Matterhorn are stunning all year round. Dine on truffles and wild mushrooms at red-checked tables: the food is Piedmontese and delicious. On the little terrace is an old bread oven that serves as a barbecue in summer… a special place run by special people.

rooms	3 + 1: 3 triples. 1 apartment for 4.
price	Half-board €60–€90 p.p.
meals	Half-board only.
closed	Never.
directions	Exit A5 St-Vincent-Chatillon for Valtournenche for 19km through Paquier & Losanche. After 5km, right for Lago Blu for 50m to hotel parking, on right. Call to be collected.

Bed & Breakfast

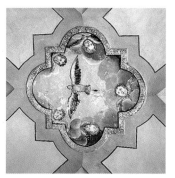

	Luca Giani	
tel	+39 333 342 0657 (mob)	
e-mail	info@baitalayet.com	
web	www.baitalayet.com	

piste or lift	1.5km
cross-country trail	3km
lift for bikes	3km
village centre	3km

Map 6 Entry 116

Hotel Hermitage
11021 Cervinia, Italy

Hidden from the the centre of village by a coppice of pine and larch, Hotel Hermitage has an almost secretive feel. At the end of the snowy drive: a small, modest entrance; inside, a smart and smiling reception. Corrado's family has been running this spectacular place for over 30 years. The restaurant is huge, but cosy alcoves, heavy curtains and soft lights lend it intimacy. The spa has a pool and a hammam, the reading room is like something out of a stately home: silver candlesticks on the mantlepiece, fine cognacs on the sideboard, wide floorboards polished with age. The standard bedrooms are wallpapered in simple designs and smartly furnished with antiques, dried flowers, framed prints, large mirrors; ceiling rafters in several rooms are impressive. The suites have warm colours, and walls lined in a simple yellow and red tartan; one is named after Edward Wymper, conqueror of the Matterhorn in 1865. Sofas are big, checked and comfortable, crystal glasses glisten, log fires smoulder and the mighty mountain fills every view.

rooms	40: 33 twins/doubles, 7 suites.
price	€ 300–€ 600. High season: half-board only, € 180–€ 350 p.p.
meals	Dinner € 60.
closed	April-June; September-November.
directions	Exit A5 St-Vincent-Chatillon for Valtournenche for 27km. At fork in Cervinia road, right for ski lift & Hermitage. Hotel up hill, 150m on right.

Hotel

piste or lift	200m
cross-country trail	1km
lift for bikes	200m
village centre	250m

	Corrado Neyroz
tel	+39 0166 948998
fax	+39 0166 949032
e-mail	hermitage@relaischateaux.com
web	www.hotelhermitage.com

Map 6 Entry 117

Hotel Mignon
Via Carrel 50, 11021 Cervinia, Italy

In the busy, modern centre of the pedestrianized high street is the Hotel Mignon. Past the cosy bar, popular with locals, to the old-fashioned reception desk above which light filters through stained-glass windows. The breakfast room is appealing with its mountain pictures, fresh flowers and generous buffet; downstairs is a smart living room with patterned sofas and lamps. Bedrooms are cosy and part-pine-clad, with new furniture, wooden floors, coordinated floral fabrics and colourful rugs; some are large, some small, some under the eaves. There's an easy atmosphere: Cristiana and her husband are ski instructors and have the knack of making you feel at home the moment you arrive. You'll eat well, too – on venison, wild mushrooms and rich pastas filled with fontina. The position is perfect in snow-sure Cervinia, lift-linked to Zermatt with a vast ski and snowboard terrain. The summer season, however, is fairly short because of the high altitude.

rooms	20: 14 twins/doubles, 3 singles, 3 triples.
price	€ 120–€ 240.
meals	Dinner € 30.
closed	May–June; September–October.
directions	A5 exit St-Vincent-Chatillon for Valtournenche for 27km to Cervinia. Left opposite Sporting Hotel. Follow road round village to far end of main street. Hotel 1st on left.

Hotel

	Family Pession
tel	+39 0166 949344
fax	+39 0166 949687
e-mail	info@mignoncervinia.com
web	www.mignoncervinia.com

piste or lift	100m
cross-country trail	100m
lift for bikes	100m
village centre	10m

Map 6   Entry 118

Les Neiges d'Antan
Loc. Cret Perreres, 11021 Cervinia, Italy

A sauna with a window and a hot tub with a Matterhorn view! Ludovico's father built this hotel because of its stupendous setting; now his son – a photographer by profession – has taken it on. Pass the logs stacked by the front door to enter a delightfully rustic and atmospherically lit stübe whose white walls are lined with vintage black and white photographs – all very traditional. Quite a surprise, then, to find such stylishly redesigned bedrooms upstairs. They are large and lovely, and come with luxurious bathrooms of stone and teak. The views are particularly impressive from the balconied rooms at the front (a pylon being the sole blemish). The large dining room is divided into sections, creating an intimate setting for some fine regional cooking from Carmen, mother and *patronne*. Cheeses, meats, hams and liquers come from small, local producers, and there are no fewer than 800 Italian and French wines waiting in the cellars. Stunning seclusion – yet the hotel's bus shuttles you to town and lifts in minutes.

rooms	24: 19 twins/doubles, 1 triple, 4 suites.
price	Half board € 70–€ 208 p.p. Suite half-board € 110–€ 290 p.p.
meals	Half-board only.
closed	May–June; September–October.
directions	Exit A5 St-Vincent-Chatillon for Valtournenche. 3km after Losanche, right on exiting 2nd tunnel. Hotel 2km.

Hotel

piste or lift	3km		
cross-country trail	3km	tel	+39 0166 948775
lift for bikes	3km	fax	+39 0166 948852
village centre	3km	e-mail	info@lesneigesdantan.it
		web	www.lesneigesdantan.it

Ludovico Bich

Map 6 Entry 119

Pankeo
Fraz. Crépin 73, 11028 Valtournenche, Italy

Mauro restores houses so was delighted when he found this 1754 barn in little Crepin. A true Italian, his attention to detail and love of authenticity run deep; he spent two years researching the wood-carving traditions of the Valle d'Aosta. As a result, he, Adelaide and their four children have created a charming and intimate place to stay. There's no dining room – instead, each bedroom has its own breakfast corner where organic breads, cheeses and jams set you up for the day. And the rooms are delightful, with their newly tiled floors, fresh white walls, country antiques, simple chairs and table decorated with pretty lace mats. There's a solarium here, and a swimming pool nearby, to which you have free entry. Valtournenche is walkable, with a thriving community; the village elders continue to play boules, and greet you as you pass. You're also quite likely to come across some lively local event – any excuse for a get-together – from des-alpage (the bringing of the cows down from the mountains for winter) to tastings of the fruity local red wine, La Grola. Utterly authentic.

rooms	3: 2 twins, 1 single.
price	€ 60–€ 80. Singles € 40.
meals	10% discount with local restaurants.
closed	First week September.
directions	A5 exit St-Vincent-Chatillon for Valtournenche for 19km; left for Crépin. Park before road narrows. 100m further, on right.

Bed & Breakfast

	Adelaide Rosset	piste or lift	100m
tel	+39 0166 92956	cross–country trail	2km
fax	+39 0166 920049	lift for bikes	10m
e-mail	rosset.adelaide@pankeo.com	village centre	900m
web	www.pankeo.com		

Map 6 Entry 120

Grandes Murailles
Via Roma 78, 11028 Valtournenche, Italy

Giuseppe and Maria Teresa's smiles, attention to detail and unselfconscious good taste have created an irresistible place to stay. The young couple also have a passion for the mountains and can advise you on everything – in impeccable English. The house sits in the middle of the village under the gaze of an old chapel, surrounded by a baker's dozen of pizzerias, hotels and shops. No sooner have you spotted the warm yellow façade than you're up the granite steps and in the door. The reception desk is a Louis XVI-style bureau and sets the scene: a feel of traditional gentleman's club (minus the cigar smoke) pervades this small hotel. Expect comfortable checked sofas, worn leather armchairs, rows of books, the crackle of logs, friendly chat and laughter. Immaculate bedrooms are large and well-proportioned, bathrooms are spotless. Oil paintings decorate the warm yellow walls, rugs cover wooden floors, carved and wrought-iron beds make up the rest. They have a little brasserie that serves regional dishes, and breakfasts are feasts. A sauna here, and a swimming pool up the road.

rooms	16: 13 twins/doubles, 1 single, 2 triples.
price	€80–€170.
meals	Dinner, by arrangement. Half-board option with local restaurants.
closed	Open all year round and weekends only, May-June & October-November.
directions	Exit A5 St-Vincent-Chatillon to Valtournenche. Hotel opposite church.

Hotel

piste or lift	800m	
cross-country trail	1km	tel
lift for bikes	800m	fax
village centre	10m	e-mail
		web

Giuseppe & Maria Teresa Fournier
tel   +39 0166 932956
fax   +39 0166 932702
e-mail info@hotelgmurailles.com
web   www.hotelgmurailles.com

Map 6 Entry 121

Hôtellerie de Mascognaz
11020 Champoluc, Italy

The thrillingly isolated Hôtellerie is reached via snowmobile in winter and 4x4 in summer. And, being perched just above Champoluc, has hours of sunshine. You enter on the first floor, up the wooden ramp once used for the animals, straight into the living room with big open fire. The 1903 village school has all the exposed stone and pine-clad walls you could wish for, and a ruggedly luxurious feel. Modern table lamps add a glow; an antique dresser is pretty with china. Across the living room is a chic bar/dining area, where booth-like tables and benches sit snugly under chunky timber eaves. The wooden floor is delightfully uneven and worn. Bedrooms are downstairs, reached via an open-rung wooden stair, cosy with low ceilings and small windows framed with heavy curtains. Wall-mounted sconces illuminate old pine, colourful carpets cheer wooden boards, fat white duvets sit on antique beds. The position of the chalet – and the neighbouring Breithorn – is remarkable… particularly if you fancy being whisked off by helicopter to Monterosa's virgin pistes. A free bus takes you to the lifts.

rooms	7 twins/doubles.
price	€90–€180 half-board p.p. Winter: €7,500–€18,000 per week (whole chalet).
meals	Half-board only. Catered in winter.
closed	15 April-May; October-November.
directions	Exit A5 Verres for Val d'Ayas for 27km to Champoluc. Hotel on right.

Hotel

	Danilo Guerrini	piste or lift	3km
tel	+39 0125 308734	cross-country trail	2.5km
fax	+39 0125 308398	lift for bikes	2.5km
e-mail	info@breithornhotel.com	village centre	3km
web	www.breithornhotel.com		

Map 6 Entry 122

Breithorn Hotel

Route Ramey 27, Ayas, 11020 Champoluc, Italy

Fairy lights are scattered among the pine trees at the entrance: it's that sort of place. Inside, a tangle of timber, every ceiling finely panelled or rustically raftered. In the living room are comfortable sofas, paintings in gilded frames and a smouldering fire. Antique pine clothes the walls of the reading room and reception areas, fine rugs cover creaking boards. The bar brims with candles. More refined rusticity in the dining room, split into several rooms and open to non-residents: expect a happy bustle and the delicious aroma of regional cooking. The hotel closed in the 1970s, fell into ruin, then rose from the ashes in 1995 when it was reinvented, courtesy of timbers from a high-pasture chalet. The original stone stair leads up to bedrooms, all different, all woody, all charming; some have a balcony, others a view. Bathrooms are colourfully contemporary with a mix of handmade tiles. There's also a delicious health spa. The old hotel, the first in the valley, has been welcoming guests for 100 years; fading photographs of distinguished mountaineers who stayed here line the walls.

rooms	31: 12 twins/doubles, 15 triples, 4 family rooms.
price	€75–€200. Winter: €200–€300.
meals	Lunch à la carte €30–€40. Dinner €40–€60.
closed	15 April-May; October-November.
directions	A5 exit Verres for Val D'Ayas for 27km to Champoluc. Hotel on right.

Hotel

piste or lift	200m		Danilo Guerrini	
cross-country trail	900m	tel	+39 0125 308734	
lift for bikes	200m	fax	+39 0125 308398	
village centre	10m	e-mail	info@breithornhotel.com	
		web	www.breithornhotel.com	

Map 6 Entry 123

Villa Anna Maria Hotel de Charme
Via Croues 5, 11020 Champoluc, Italy

A fine 1940s villa built of neat round logs on a raised slope, a few minutes' walk from the village through tall pines and scrunching snow. (Staff carry your bags from the hotel car park to the house – lucky you.) In summer, relax on a red deckchair in sloping gardens to be serenaded by the birds. Floors, walls and high ceilings are darkly wooden; antiques, books and a piano make it homely. The breakfast room stretches before you, its tall glass windows pulling in the light; houseplants give it an elegant conservatory feel. At the top of a fine wooden staircase bedrooms await, some large, some less so; all are different, all dotted with antiques. Rag rugs brighten the floors, red and white gingham curtains frame the windows. A delicious aroma wafts through from the kitchen downstairs thanks to Grandma's recipes; ham roulardes stuffed with fontina cheese are a speciality. Miki and son Jean Noël speak perfect English, are proud of the family house and look after you beautifully. The resort of Champoluc is delightful, informal and old-fashioned; some villagers still wear wooden clogs.

rooms	20: 11 twins/doubles, 2 singles, 5 triples, 2 quadruples.
price	€ 146–€ 180. Half-board € 48–€ 80 p.p.
meals	Lunch € 15. Dinner € 20.
closed	Never.
directions	Exit A5 Verres for Val d'Ayas for 27km to Champoluc. 1st right after pharmacy; after 2 bends, right into hotel car park, signed. Staff will help carry bags.
Hotel	

	Miki & Jean Noël Origone	piste or lift	300m
tel	+39 0125 307128	cross–country trail	500m
fax	+39 0125 307984	lift for bikes	250m
e-mail	hotelannamaria@tiscali.it	village centre	100m
web	www.hotelvillaannamaria.com		

Map 6 Entry 124

Gasthaus Lysjoch
11020 Gressoney La Trinité, Italy

You are almost at the end of the Gressoney valley... yet the lifts that sweep you into the Monterosa ski bowl lie outside the door (as do the pistes). They speak German in these villages and the area has an Austrian feel. Inside the guesthouse, dark mottled marble on the floors, light pine on the walls and, in the sitting area, pine benches and floral sofas and chairs. Rustic cow bells, ancient bridles and mountain landscapes add interest to the walls. The restaurant is old-fashioned with its carved pine benches and brass overhead lights, while bedrooms have a 1970s feel and dark carpeting, but are cosily lit. Built-in cupboards provide plenty of hanging space, bedspreads add colour, shower rooms are just fine; some bedrooms have had a modern refit. Signor Dante senior built the hotel 30 years ago and it is still family-run. Come for acres of virgin snow in winter, hiking in summer and an amazing, off-the-beaten-track sensation. You could be in the middle of nowhere, yet a smattering of shops and bars lies up the road.

rooms	12: 5 doubles, 5 twins/doubles, 2 singles.
price	Half-board €50-€75 p.p.
meals	Half-board only.
closed	May & October-November.
directions	Exit A5 Pont St Martin for Val di Gressoney. Hotel 1.2km past Gressoney la Trinité, on right.

Hotel

piste or lift	50m	
cross-country trail	50m	tel
lift for bikes	1.2km	fax
village centre	300m	e-mail
		web

	Signor Dante
tel	+39 0125 366150
fax	+39 0125 366365
e-mail	hillyslsjoch@hotellyslsjoch.com
web	www.hotellyslsjoch.com

Map 6 Entry 125

Maso Doss
38086 Madonna di Campiglio, Italy

Trees shade the empty, bumpy road down to the old farm. Dried corn hangs on racks against the weathered façade, a spindly balcony traverses the traditional base, and you enter at the back. Dining and sitting rooms are big, ceilings sweep to the eaves, beams cross high above your head, and farm tools and rustic bits and pieces add to the character. Rest awhile on the red-cushioned benches that front the huge open fire and settle down to a hot mug of chocolate, or a delicious glass of Pinot Bianco. There's a sauna, too, and a magnificent panelled stübe, its dresser filled with local china. Muslin curtains frame small windows; behind is a balcony with Dolomite views. Bedrooms are traditional and cosy, antique beds have sheets hand-embroidered by Signora. The food is excellent and seasonal: fungi and venison in autumn, local cheeses for a picnic, vegetables and salads from the garden. Hire bikes or skis and set off from the door. Climbing, mountain biking, skiing and more — all is possible from Madonna di Campiglio, and the resort is as swish as Cortina — just smaller.

rooms	6 twins/doubles.
price	Half-board €70–€130 p.p.; €330–€760 p.p. per week.
meals	Half- or full-board only.
closed	Rarely.
directions	From A22 exit Trento Centro, right on N45 for Sarche & Madonna di C. Right on N237 for Tione. Right on N239 for Pinzolo. Right after S. Antonio di Mavignola, follow signs.

Catered

	Fam. Caola
tel	+39 0465 502758
fax	+39 0465 502311
e-mail	info@masodoss.com
web	www.masodoss.com

piste or lift	6km
cross-country trail	200m
lift for bikes	10m
village centre	1km

Map 2 Entry 126

Bio-hotel Hermitage
Via Castelletto Inferiore 63, 38084 Madonna di Campiglio, Italy

It's not often that a bio-hotel comes with such a splash of luxury. Built a century ago, the old Hermitage has been entirely refashioned – with a modern 'eco' eye and a flourish of decorative turret. A wooden floor spans the reception area; behind is a vast and comfortable living room. A Tyrolean-tiled woodburner dominates the centre; windows open onto a balcony with the best views in the Alps. You eat at red-clothed tables on Trentino dishes and homemade pasta in the stübe, with its lovely panelled ceiling of old, recycled wood. The main restaurant is larger but as beautiful. Bedrooms are serene, some are under the eaves, most have a balcony and the suites are huge. Wooden floors are softened by Persian rugs or pale carpets from Argentina, curtains and bedspreads are prettily checked. There's a superb wellness centre and an indoor pool with a ceiling that sparkles. Bars and chic boutiques are a 10-minute walk, and the hotel has its own bus that shuttles you to the slopes. Santa tips up at Christmas distributing presents for the children from a little cabin at the end of the garden.

rooms	27: 21 twins/doubles, 6 suites for 3-4.
price	Half-board €70-€205 p.p.
meals	Half-board only.
closed	May & October-November.
directions	Exit A22 St Mich & Mezz for Madonna di Campiglio for 75km; Madonna bypass through mountain; next exit. Hotel signed on left.

Hotel

piste or lift	1.5km	
cross-country trail	2km	
lift for bikes	1.5km	
village centre	1.3km	

	Barbara Maffei
tel	+39 0465 441558
fax	+39 0465 441618
e-mail	info@biohotelhermitage.it
web	www.biohotelhermitage.it

Map 2 Entry 127

Hotel Cavallino D'Oro
Piazza Kraus 1, 39040 Castelrotto, Italy

The Little Gold Horse has been welcoming travellers since 1393. The village is postcard Tyrolean, with whitewashed or painted houses and local dress and customs still very much alive. The market runs every Friday in the summer months, the farmers setting up their stalls at the foot of the imposing 18th-century bell tower. Rooms at the inn – some facing the mountain, some the square – have a fascinating mix of beds: some painted, some four-poster, some both. Doors come painted too, as do beams in the muted green and peach sitting room. Breakfast is in a wood-dressed dining room with geraniums at the window and bright check tablecloths; all is gleaming and spotless. Hosts Susanna and Stefan are as friendly as they are efficient, organising regular concerts and a sitar at dinner. Come in summer for swimming, walking or cycling; in winter for sleigh rides, cross-country skiing (from the door) and alpine magic. There's an all-year-round wellness centre in the converted cellars, and Alpe di Siusi is a free, 20-minute bus ride away.

rooms	18: 5 doubles, 2 twins, 4 singles, 4 triples, 3 suites.
price	€80. Singles €50. Suites €100.
meals	Dinner €20–€30.
closed	November.
directions	From A22, exit for Bolzano Nord. Castelrotto signed at exit. Hotel in market square in town centre.

Hotel

	Susanna & Stefan Urthaler
tel	+39 0471 706337
fax	+39 0471 707172
e-mail	cavallino@cavallino.it
web	www.cavallino.it

piste or lift	9km
cross-country trail	100m
lift for bikes	20m
village centre	10m

Map 3 Entry 128

Sule-Hof
Streda Nevel 83, 39046 Ortisei-Val Gardena, Italy

Serious hikers adore it here. Casual walkers like it too – and skiers of all denominations. The spruce little chalet rests in a sunny valley surrounded by Dolomite views; who wouldn't feel the enchantment? Grandmother and hostess Signora Demetz has adapted her home into a charming, mountain-simple B&B. You breakfast in the wooden stübe, warmed by a ceramic stove, on homemade jams and muesli. The bedrooms are light and airy, furnished with shiny modern pine, floral fabrics and shower rooms; the apartments are traditional and homely. The smaller has a panelled ceiling and a tiled stove; the bigger tucks under the eaves, and is excellently equipped. You have an open garden for summer, a pond teeming with fish, a play area for the children, table tennis for you. Sit on the raised terrace, summer or winter, and soak up the sun and the views. Sometimes there are barbecue nights, and, in winter, dumplings all round! Ortisei, with shops, restaurants and pool, is a six-minute walk and a hop on the shuttle. *Minimum stay three nights.*

rooms	4+2: 4 doubles. 2 apartments: 1 for 2-3; 1 for 4-6.
price	€42-€60. Apt for 3 €400-€700 per week; for 6 €590-€1,130.
meals	Restaurants 5-10 minutes' walk.
closed	Rarely.
directions	A22 to Chiusa; Klausen & Gröden exit (Chiusa & Val Gardena), valley road signposted; 20 mins to Ortisei.

Bed & Breakfast

piste or lift	1km	
cross-country trail	2km	
village centre	1km	

	Roman Demetz
tel	+39 0471 797416
fax	+39 0471 797416
e-mail	sule@val-gardena.com
web	www.sule-hof.com

Map 3 Entry 129

Ciastel Colz
Strasse Marin 80, 39030 La Villa, Italy

Enter a fairy tale. An impenetrable wall with round turrets (wherein fine bedrooms lie) protects a beautiful square keep; an ancient portcullis with less ancient entry phone leads to a courtyard with pretty fruit trees and perfectly stacked logs. Inside: a long corridor with white vaulted ceiling, stone floors, antique Persian rugs... then up a stone stair, lit by lamps on wooden chests and halogen uplighters to catch every detail, from the fascinating 16th-century graffiti to the blackened walls of the smokery (the area is famous for its smoked meats). The dining rooms announce both gastronomic and regional menus, everything is homemade and delicious down to the bread and there's a wine-stacked cellar where the dungeons once were. Three of the four rooms are in the towers along the defensive outer wall; the King's Room is in the keep, on the top floor. Each room is as simply beautiful as the next with ample space and impressive attention to detail. Peer out of the small defensive window and arrow slits to the mighty peaks of the Marmolada and beyond. Unforgettable.

rooms	4: 2 doubles, 2 suites for 3.
price	€176–€270.
meals	Dinner €35–€100.
closed	April-May; October-November.
directions	S242 to Selva for 3km; S243 for Corvara for 15km to T-junction. Left for La Villa & Stern for 4.5km; left for 100m. Inn on right, signed.

Hotel

	S Wieser	
tel	+39 0471 847511	
fax	+39 0471 847511	
e-mail	colz@siriolagroup.it	
web	www.siriolagroup.it	

piste or lift	200m
cross-country trail	1km
lift for bikes	200m
village centre	400m

Map 3 Entry 130

Rosa Alpina
Strada Micura de Ru 20, 39030 San Cassiano, Italy

The mountain village of San Cassiano has 750 inhabitants – and a typical history of agri-tourism. In its heart sits the Rosa Alpina, in the Pizzinini family for 60 years. The 20-room guest house of old has become a luxury, 55-bedroom hotel with a list of accolades as long as your arm. And though it looks grand from the front, with its fairytale turrets and arrow-slit windows overlooking the valley, from the back it resembles two pretty alpine chalets that blend into the village. The two (almost) life-sized antique carved angels that greet you as you enter, old and worn yet enchanting, are a typically exquisite detail, and there are many more: simple, striking pieces, new and antique, offset by swathes of beautiful natural fabrics in off-whites and creams. Art extends to the St Hubertus restaurant where the chef's five-course feasts have netted him a Michelin star. So you are as spoiled as it is possible to be – fine linen on the beds, exquisite dishes on the table, aromatic candles in the beauty and health spa, and a free shuttle to whisk you to the slopes. Superb.

rooms	55: 34 twins/doubles, 9 triples, 12 suites for 3.
price	€85–€260.
meals	Dinner €35–€87.
closed	April-May; October-November.
directions	3km after Selva, S243 for Corvara; 15km; at T-junc, left for La Villa & Stern; 4.5km; right for San Cassiano. Head for village centre; hotel on right.

Hotel

piste or lift	300m		Hugo Pizzinini
cross-country trail	300m	tel	+39 0471 849500
lift for bikes	300m	fax	+39 0471 849377
village centre	10m	e-mail	info@rosalpina.it
		web	www.rosalpina.it

Map 3   Entry 131

Hotel Villa Stefania
Via Duca Tassilo 16, 39038 San Candido, Italy

In one of gentle San Candido's quietest and greenest corners is this villa turned small hotel. The old part of the house, pale-walled with dark red carpeting underfoot, has a grand feel, while the bedroom-filled extension is almost Japanese in mood. The lounge has flowery wallpaper and white-cushioned wicker armchairs; another room has an upright piano and lots of dark wood. In the bedroom suites, light paper walls divide the roomy living section from the comfortable, new-pine, four-poster bed. Pale polished pine floors are softened by oriental carpets; new picture windows are prettified by translucent curtains with a red floral print. Food here is contemporary Italian, delicious local meat and fish beautifully presented on white china in a blond-wood-wrapped dining room. Big windows look onto the large and well-groomed lawn with neatly arranged sunloungers shaded by willow trees – charming in summer. No pool, but you have unlimited use of the new Acquafun next door. In winter the skiing is a treat, and the lifts seldom have queues.

rooms	24: 22 twins/doubles, 2 family rooms/suites.
price	€ 53-€ 102 p.p.
meals	Half-board option: extra € 10 p.p.
closed	May & October.
directions	Exit A27 Belluno for Pian di Vedoia; S51 for Pieve di Cadore. After Cortina, right on S49 for San Candido; 2nd exit for village centre; 150m on left.

Hotel

	Mary Ortner	piste or lift	400m
tel	+39 0474 913588	cross-country trail	150m
fax	+39 0474 916255	lift for bikes	10m
e-mail	info@villastefania.com	village centre	150m
web	www.villastefania.com		

Map 3 Entry 132

Hotel Orso Grigio / Grauer Bar
Via Rainer 2, 39038 San Candido, Italy

The magnificent townhouse opposite the church has been opening its doors to visitors for 250 years; the Ladinser family goes back even further. The stripey-awned hotel has a good central position on a pedestrianized high street stuffed with market stalls and little shops. The beautiful, white-vaulted ceiling of the hotel entrance is supported by carved granite columns; little has changed structurally over the years, as you can see from the pictures and prints on the walls. But the place has certainly gone up in the world: not a stick of rickety furniture remains. Bedrooms are up a floor and come in two styles. 'Superior' rooms are furnished in light new pine, with large beds and soft duvets, and enough space for a small seating area with a glass coffee table. 'Standard' rooms have the odd antique – carpets and chairs are a touch worn but there's plenty of character and the beds are good. Old timbers and stones, the odd suit of armour... history seeps from every pore. The cooking is excellent, the family delightful and the sauna soothes weary limbs.

rooms	24: 19 twins/doubles, 5 triples.
price	Half-board € 50–€ 120 p.p.
meals	Half-board only.
closed	April-May; October-November.
directions	From Belluno, 30km east (S49). Hotel in centre, next to church.

Hotel

piste or lift	300m
cross-country trail	300m
lift for bikes	400m
village centre	10m

Martine Ladinser

tel	+39 0474 913115
fax	+39 0474 914182
e-mail	info@orsohotel.it
web	www.orsohotel.it

Map 3 Entry 133

Parkhotel Sole Paradiso
Innichen, 39038 San Candido, Italy

Move aside for the black Saint Bernard. There's a family mood here, and you sense it the moment you arrive – though many a distinguished visitor has crossed the entrance hall's Persian-rugged parquet. On the edge of a huge pine forest, the building is an 1882 tribute to Viennese imperial-style architecture. The dining room and breakfast rooms are warmly lit by retro ceiling lights, Tyrolean desserts line the buffet and dinners are feasts. Sweep up the grand staircase to 44 themed bedrooms, each different, each luxurious; choose from standard, standard with balcony, superior or royal. Styles range from late-19th-century (with four-posters) to roaring 1920s, retro 70s to contemporary 'cutting edge'. All have the softest duvets and the sweetest linen. Such attention to detail is the legacy of four generations of Ortners: these perfectionist owners take pride in getting it right. You have an indoor pool with solarium, tennis, table tennis and billiards, there's a private shuttle to the slopes (wonderfully uncrowded in the Alta Pusteria) and cross-country skiing starts from the door.

rooms	44: 32 twins, 4 four-posters, 4 singles, 4 triples.
price	Half-board €64–€110 p.p.
meals	Half-board only.
closed	April-May; October-November.
directions	From S51, 28km past Cortina right on S49 for San Candido. Hotel on left, 50m after village, towards Sexten.

Hotel

	Linda Ortner	piste or lift	200m
tel	+39 0474 913120	cross-country trail	10m
fax	+39 0474 913193	lift for bikes	200m
e-mail	info@soleparadiso.com	village centre	200m
web	www.sole-paradiso.com		

Map 3 Entry 134

Berghotel Tirol
Helmweg, Via Monte Elmo 10, 39030 Sesto/Sexten, Italy

Nature trails and ski runs start from the door. The hotel sits on its hillside gazing imperiously onto the Dolomites and the village below. You have a twinning of chalets here, the older one sitting in front of the lighter extension and linked by a semi-circular glazed restaurant with sensational views. Food is the best of traditional regional; the hotel's list of activities is long. You get an impressive indoor pool with a vaulted ceiling, table tennis, billiards and a playroom for tots, a shuttle to the lifts, mountain bikes, children's bike seats and a spa with every treatment under the sun. All you'd hope for, for the price – and plenty of Tyrolean charm in the sitting room with its open fire, rugs on polished boards, books, pictures and the odd antler mounted on the wall. Bedrooms are posh affairs, with balconies and big views. Walls are crépy-white, ceilings new-beamed, walls carpeted or pine, windows framed by long drapes. There's a well-kept garden, a cobbled drive and a small pond, great for kids in summer. For market bustle, pop into the village of Moso.

rooms	36: 23 twins/doubles, 10 quadruples, 3 suites.
price	Half-board € 64-€ 119 p.p.
meals	Half-board only.
closed	April; November.
directions	From S51, 28km past Cortina, right on S49 for San Candido; right for Sexten. Hotel signed in village.

Hotel

piste or lift	100m		Walter Holzer
cross-country trail	100m	tel	+39 0474 710386
lift for bikes	50m	fax	+39 0474 710455
village centre	150m	e-mail	info@berghotel.com
		web	www.berghotel.com

Map 3   Entry 135

Lago Ghedina
Locanda Lago Ghedina, 32043 Cortina d'Ampezzo, Italy

The setting is perhaps one of the loveliest in the Alps – worthy of at least one film crew. (Cortina has hosted a stream of feature films as well as a winter Olympics.) Picture an exquisite, crystal-clear lake teeming with trout, the Dolomites mirrored in its waters, larch and pine trees all around, and a softly pitched chalet at the far end. Step in to a delicious setting for delicious regional food: the raftered restaurant with rooms, atmospherically furnished with rustic pieces and antique farm tools, has a vast hay rack below which rows of crisp white tables twinkle with polished glass and silver. Fish is a speciality and the wine list is long. Upstairs are the bedrooms, three with a rough-hewn mezzanine and a ladder to a bed under the eaves – fresh cotton sheets and fat duvets are worth the last climb of the day. Lago Ghedina sits by its lake at the end of a long winding road and there's not a sound to disturb you – only the call of the ptarmigan and the wind stirring the trees. The ski lifts are a short drive.

rooms	6: 2 doubles, 1 double with sofabed, 3 family.
price	€80-€150.
meals	Dinner from €28.
closed	Open all year and Fri-Sun only May-June; October-November.
directions	From A27 for Belluno exit at Pian di Vedoia for Pieve di Cadore on S51. 4km after Cortina d'Ampezzo, left for Lago Ghedina. 3km on right.

Bed & Breakfast

	Stefano Pompananin	piste or lift	3km
tel	+39 0436 860876	cross-country trail	3km
fax	+39 0436 860876	lift for bikes	4km
e-mail	lagoghedina@cortinadampezzo.it	village centre	4km
web	www.cortinadampezzo.it/lagoghedina		

Map 3 Entry 136

Hotel Menardi
Via Majou 110, 32043 Cortina d'Ampezzo, Italy

With its key position, on the Imperial Royal Street of Alemagne leading to the Cimabanche Pass, the 1836 farmhouse was not going to stay un-noticed for very long. Soon the hay rooms evolved into guest rooms, then become World War I barracks... eventually the fine old place was returned to the family and the Menardi brothers (a charming pair) created the hotel that you see today. Clocks, dowry chests, Persian carpets and rows of cowbells are just some of the things that fill the reading and sitting rooms – along with Darwinian-style flora and fauna prints and black and white photographs on pristine walls. Some of the bedrooms are in a separate chalet; those upstairs have knotted pine furniture and carpeted floors. Big windows look onto the Dolomite peaks; double-glazing protects you from traffic sounds and winter chill. Outside, ancient gnarled fruit trees adorn whitewashed walls; loungers dot the lovely, larch-filled gardens in summer. Grand Cortina, Pearl of the Dolomites, is Italian to its core; its winter slopes are deserted until mid-morning as winter visitors loll in bed.

rooms	51: 41 twins/doubles, 5 triples, 5 doubles.
price	€90–€200.
meals	Lunch €15–€30. Dinner €20.
closed	Mid-April-mid-May; mid-September-mid-December.
directions	From A27 for Belluno, exit at Pian di Vedoia for Pieve di Cadore on S51. Hotel on right, 2km after Cortina d'Ampezzo.

Hotel

piste or lift	1.5km		Sig. Antonio Menardi
cross-country trail	3km	tel	+39 0436 2400
lift for bikes	2km	fax	+39 0436 862183
village centre	2km	e-mail	info@hotelmenardi.it
		web	www.hotelmenardi.it

Map 3   Entry 137

Hotel de la Poste
Piazza Roma 14, 32043 Cortina d'Ampezzo, Italy

It was once the post office, not surprisingly – and the old post office counter makes a magnificent bar. The warm yellow exterior of the Poste – its balconies aflame with geraniums in summer – faces a large cobbled square in the elegantly pedestrianised centre; spot the fur coats and the Gucci poochies on parade before dinner. Inside: wide arching corridors and diamond-patterned marble floors, and public rooms reminiscent of a grand city hotel – busy wallpapers, fine tapestries, thick drapes and vast chandeliers. There's more of a charming chalet feel to the polished all-wood stübe (this part of Italy used to be Austrian Tyrol), while the sitting room sports a modern open fire, house plants, coordinated armchairs and glass ashtrays on doilies. Every different bedroom tells a story, its framed black and white photographs recording the Poste's triumphs and tribulations down the years. The Manaigo family has been taking in guests since 1835 and the current generation couldn't be nicer.

rooms	76: 48 twins/doubles, 25 singles, 3 suites for 2-4.
price	€ 189–€ 346. Singles € 126–€ 189.
meals	Dinner € 38–€ 74.
closed	After Easter-12 June; October-20 December.
directions	Exit A27 Belluno for Pian di Vedoia; S51 for Pieve di Cadore. Follow 1-way system in Cortina, back towards Pieve di C. On left, opp. tourist office.
Hotel	

	Gottardo Manaigo	piste or lift	500m
tel	+39 0436 4271	cross-country trail	1km
fax	+39 0436 868435	lift for bikes	500m
e-mail	info@delaposte.it	village centre	10m
web	www.delaposte.it		

Map 3 Entry 138

Winter sports and the environment

Low-cost airlines, the short break culture and freedom of travel have helped 'liberate' us all. But at what cost? Although winter and summer tourism has undoubtedly injected new life into traditional farming communities, our holidays are having a greater impact on the environment than we sometimes care to imagine. The larger, all-inclusive hotel complexes tend to neglect local communities by importing facilities and giving little back; cars and planes pollute; and developing resorts often damage the fragile beauty of the areas that drew visitors there in the first place.

Nowhere is global warming more noticeable than in the Alps. Glaciers are retreating, the tree line is rising and the seasons are becoming more unpredictable. In response, resorts have employed increasingly sophisticated methods to keep the lucrative snow on their slopes, with artificial snow cannons, matting and fences all helping lengthen the season. But the mountain ecosystem is a fragile one and human intervention has created a disturbing imbalance - tons of water are used in snowmaking, growing extremes of temperature (from 40C in the summer to -30C in the winter) have led to increased ice falls and crumbling rocks, and deforestation of pistes has encouraged landslides. High altitude flora takes a long time to reestablish itself in these areas, and skiers are increasingly going off-piste into the winderness, clipping bushes and trees and disturbing wildlife. A greater awareness of sustainability is urgently needed.

But it's not all gloom and doom. Studies have been commissioned by some of the larger ski areas and dedicated nature reserves have been set up with stiff penalties for skiers who enter them. In recent years the purpose-built resorts have had to adapt to consumer demand for more traditional settings and huge numbers of trees have been reintroduced, along with wildlife. Very strict guidelines now govern

Photo above Mike Richardson
Photo opposite Nick Woodford

new developments and the frantic expansion of the super resorts is at last slowing down. There are also some unusual local laws to be aware of. Picking mountain flowers, mushrooms or berries is often forbidden, especially in national parks, while some Swiss by-laws dictate that at certain times one cannot wash dishes or flush the loo.

Our guide books delight in independent travel, which tends to benefit small communities and increases communication and understanding. We aim to encourage travellers to think of the silent effect they are having on the world.

If you are interested in exploring these issues you might contact Tourism Concern, campaigners for ethical and fair-trade tourism. Tel: 020 7133 3330; www.tourismconcern.org.uk

National holidays...

in Austria:
April 27 Second Republic Day
May 15 National Day
October 26 – National Holiday of Austria
November 12 Republic Day

in France:
May 8, Liberation Day
May 5, 2005 Ascension
May 15, 2005 Pentecost
May 16, 2005 Whit Monday
July 14 Bastille Day
November 11 Armistice Day

in Italy:
January 6 Epiphany
April 25 Liberation Day
December 8 Feast of the Immaculate

in Switzerland:
January 2 Berchtold's Day
February 6, 2005 – First Sunday in February: Homstrom
April 7, 2005 – First Thursday in April: Glarus Festival
April 30 May Day Eve
August 1 Independence Day

... and general holidays:
January 1 New Year's Day (*Neues Jahr; Jour de l'An; Capo d'Anno*)
March 27, 2005 Easter
May 1 Labour Day
August 15 Assumption of the Virgin
November 1 All Saints Day

Mountain Activities

Always check that your instructors are qualified, and that your insurance covers adventure and outdoor sports. These are some of the things you can get up to in the mountains.

In summer

Bungee jumping – falling from bridges, cranes or cable-cars with elastic attached to ankles

Climbing and abseiling - climbs and descents on specific routes, using specialist equipment

Trekking with llamas – following mountain tracks on foot, llamas carrying your bags

Hydrospeeding – swimming behind a pointed polystyrene float down rapids in a thick wetsuit

Canyoning – abseiling down waterfalls

Parapenting – running from a steep slope with a parachute and gently gliding to earth

Delta planing – running from a steep slope with a fixed wing and gently gliding to earth

In winter

Alpine or downhill skiing

Off-piste or backcountry skiing – skiing on virgin snow

Cross-country skiing – free-heel skiing on skinny skis, along undulating tracks

Snowboarding – feet attached sideways onto a board used for jumps and carving downhill

Telemarking - off-track, more extreme version of cross-country skiing, skier bending knee on turn

Ski touring – climbing mountains with specialised skis and skins and skiing back down

Mono-skiing – feet attached parallel to a single downhill ski

Ice-climbing – using ice axes, crampons and other specialised equipment to scale ice falls

Ice-diving – scuba-diving, in thick wetsuit, through frozen lakes and swimming under the ice

Snow-mobile tours – using a motorised sled to cover large distances into the wilderness

Curling – hurling heavy stones with handles towards a target on ice

Snowshoeing – using shoes clipped to special rackets; a niche but growing sport

Photo above Sara Hay

Ski Piste Classification – Skiers
Safety Code
Skiing can be enjoyed in many
ways. At ski areas you may see
people using alpine, snowboard,
telemark, cross-country and other
specialised ski equipment, such as
that used by disabled skiers.

Regardless of how you decide to
enjoy the slopes, always show
courtesy to others and be aware
that there are elements of risk in
skiing that common sense and
personal awareness can help
reduce. Observe the points listed
below and share with other skiers
the responsibility for a great skiing
experience.

1. Always stay in control.

2. Remember people ahead of you
have the right of way.

3. When stopping, choose a safe
place for you and others.

4. Whenever starting downhill or
merging, look uphill and downhill
and yield.

5. Use breaks or a snowboard leash
to help prevent runaway equipment.

6. Observe signs and warnings, and
keep off closed pistes.

7. Know how to use the lifts safely.

Standard European Ski Piste
Classification
Green – beginner easy
Blue – intermediate easy
Red – intermediate difficult
Black – expert difficult

Photo above Nick Woodford
Photo opposite Alex King-Sorrell

Ski Club of Great Britain

Special offer: two days' skiing with a Ski Club rep

If you book your special place to stay through this guide, and the local resort is one of 33 where Ski Club reps are based, you can ski with the local rep for two days in that resort, free of charge. You might then want to take advantage of the Alpine join scheme which offers two years' membership for the price of one.

This offer applies to these resorts:

France	Entry numbers
• Alpe d'Huez	69 • 70 • 71
• La Plagne/ Les Arcs	55

Austria	
• Kitzbühel	15
• Obergurgl	8
• Zell am See	21 • 22

Italy	
• Madonna di Campiglio	126 • 127

Switzerland	
• Klosters/Davos	96 • 97 • 98
• Saas Fee	94
• St Moritz	100 • 101 • 102
• Zermatt/Cervinia	91 • 92 • 93
116 • 117 • 118 • 119 • 120 • 121	

Photo above Henry Dallal
Photo opposite John Norris

Special membership offer
for Special Places readers

The Ski Club of Great Britain is now over 100 years old. With the knowledge we have built up over the last 100 years, we are looking forward to taking the club forward into the next one hundred.

Why not take advantage of the great offer we are giving to readers of this issue of *Special Places to Stay Mountains of Europe*, for Membership to the Ski Club of Great Britain?

Everyone who joins the club using the code below will be sent a free copy of Arnie Wilson's book *Top Ski Resorts of the World*. This book is a beautiful hardback 'coffee table' book with great descriptions and stunning photography of the resorts Arnie feels are the best in the world. A great addition to any snow lover's living room.

Membership costs:
- for an individual £50
- for families £71

As a member, you will receive hundreds of benefits and discounts that are unavailable elsewhere, including:
- Savings of between 5% and 15% on holidays booked with over 60 tour operators
- Comprehensive on- and off-piste insurance cover
- Skiing and boarding with Ski Club reps in over 40 premier resorts in Europe and North America
- Access to the Club's Information Department, an unbiased and invaluable resource to help you make the right decision on every aspect of snowsports
- Discounts and offers from outlets including Snow + Rock, Blacks, Ellis Brigham and hundreds of local independent snowsports retailers (for full listings see web site)
- Annual subscription to *Ski and Board*, the Club magazine (four issues)
- Access to advice on independent travel and deals on trains, transfers and ferries.

To set up your membership, please call the Ski Club's Membership Department on 0845 45 807 82 or log on to skiclub.co.uk and quote 'SPTS1'.

Ski Club of Great Britain,
The White House,
57-63 Church Road,
Wimbledon SW19 5SB
Tel: 020 8410 2000
Fax 020 8410 2001
www.skiclub.co.uk

Terms and Conditions. This offer is restricted to new members only and is subject to the completion of a Direct Debit for subsequent year's membership. This offer expires on 30th September 2006.

Which airport for which resort

The closest airport is given first, followed by any other feasible alternatives. The closest airport is not necessarily in the same country as the resort.

Alpbach
Innsbruck or Salzburg
Alpe d'Huez
Lyon
Arosa
Zurich
Bad Gastein
Salzburg
Bourg Saint Maurice
Chambery or Lyon or Geneva
Breuil Cervinia
Geneva or Turin or Milan
Briancon
Lyon or Turin
Grand Massif
Geneva
Chamonix Valley
Geneva
Champoluc
Geneva or Turin or Milan
Chateau-d'Oex
Geneva
Cogne
Geneva or Turin or Milan
Cortina d'Ampezzo
Venice
Courchevel
Chambery or Lyon or Geneva
Courmayeur
Geneva or Turin or Milan
Crans-Montana
Sion or Geneva

Davos
Zurich
Flims-Laax
Zurich
Gressoney La Trinite
Turin or Milan
Grindelwald
Zurich or Basel or Geneva
Gstaad
Geneva
Innsbruck
Innsbruck
Ischgl & Galtur
Innsbruck or Zurich
Kandersteg
Zurich or Geneva or Basel
Kaprun
Salzburg
Kitzbuhel
Munich
Klosters
Zurich
Kuhtai
Innsbruck

Photo above Alex King-Sorrell

La Clusaz
Geneva
Les Arcs / La Plagne
Chambery or Lyon or Geneva
La Grave
Lyon or Turin
La Thuile
Geneva or Turin or Milan
La Villa
Verona or Venice
Le Grand Bornand
Geneva
Lech
Zurich or Innsbruck
Les Contamines
Geneva
Les Gets
Geneva
Les Saises
Chambery or Geneva or Lyon
Madonna di Campiglio
Verona
Massif des Aravis
Geneva
Megève
Geneva
Meribel
Chambery or Geneva or Lyon
Morzine
Geneva
Mürren
Zurich or Basel or Geneva
Obergurgl
Innsbruck
Saas Fee
Sion or Geneva
Samoens
Geneva
San Candido

Venice or Verona
San Cassiano
Venice or Verona
Sauze D'Oulx
Turin
Serre Chevalier
Lyon or Turin
St Anton
Innsbruck or Zurich
St Mortiz
Zurich
St Ulrich
Verona or Venice
Ste Foy Tarentaise
Chambery or Lyon or Geneva
Val d'Isère
Chambery or Lyon or Geneva
Valmorel
Chambery or Lyon or Geneva
Verbier
Sion or Geneva
Villars
Sion or Geneva
Wengen
Zurich or Basel or Geneva
Zell am See
Salzburg
Zermatt
Sion or Geneva

Photo opposite Allys Williams

Major flight routes

These routes are direct but may be weekly or several times a day; check on the airlines' web sites. Several cities have several airports, usually at some distance from the city centre. Please check with the airline in question. Routings may change during the lifetime of this guide.

Switzerland
Geneva
Swiss Air from Heathrow & London City
Easyjet from Gatwick, Luton, Liverpool & East Midlands
BMI Baby from Cardiff, East Midlands, Manchester & Teeside
BA from Heathrow, London City, Gatwick & Manchester
Flybe from Southampton, Jersey, Guernsey & Dublin

Photo above Mike Richardson

Sion
Swiss Air from Heathrow

Zurich
Swiss Air from Heathrow, London City & Manchester
Easyjet from Gatwick & Luton
BA from Heathrow & Manchester

France
Lyon
Easyjet from Stansted
BA from Heathrow & Manchester
Ryanair from Stansted

Chambery
Flybe from Southampton

Austria
Salzburg
Ryanair from Stansted
Flybe from Birmingham & Southampton

Basel
Easyjet from Liverpool & Stansted
Swiss Air from Heathrow & Manchester
BA from Heathrow

Italy
Milan
Easyjet from Gatwick & Stansted
Ryanair air from Luton & Stansted
Bmi Baby from East Midlands & Cardiff
BA from Heathrow & Manchester
Alitalia from Heathrow &

Manchester

Turin
Ryanair from Stansted
BA from Gatwick

Verona
Ryanair from Stansted
BA from Gatwick

Venice
Easyjet from Bristol, East Midlands
& Stansted
Ryanair from Stansted
BA from Gatwick & Manchester

Germany
Innsbruck
Austrian Airlines from Heathrow
(& Manchester on charter)

Munich
Easyjet from Stansted
BA from Heathrow
Lufthansa from Heathrow &
Manchester
Many airlines no longer take
bookings by telephone; their web
sites are listed below.
Easyjet – www.easyjet.com
Bmi baby – www.bmibaby.com
Ryanair – www.ryanair.com
Flybe – www.flybe.com
Swiss – www.swiss.com
British Airways – www.ba.com
Air France – www.airfrance.com
Alitalia – www.alitalia.com
Lufthansa – www.lufthansa.com
Austrian Airlines – www.aua.com

Photo opposite Nick Woodford

Glossary

A few foreign words used in our write-ups:

French
Mazot – small chalet or hut, traditionally used to store food
Crépy – rendered walls, usually white with a rough textured finish
Gîte – self-catering apartment/house
Alpage – high mountain pastures
Des-alpage – bringing the livestock down from the mountain at the end of the summer
Sapin – pine tree
Refuge – mountain hut where skiers and walkers take shelter, and may be fed and lodged
Aiguille – needle (as in mountain peaks)
Vin chaud – mulled wine
Ski de fond – cross-country skiing
Télécabine – ski lift

German
Stübe – traditional wood-panelled dining room
Schloss – castle
Gasthof – family-run hotel or guesthouse

Italian
Grappa – a strong grape-based liqueur, like brandy
Genepi – a bittersweet liqueur made from the genepi flower
Antipasti – starter plate of meats, cheeses and olives served with bread sticks
Torcetti – rich butter biscuits
Lago – lake
Osteria – traditional wood-panelled restaurant

Photo above Nick Woodford

Resort Tourist offices

Resort Tourist Offices
For piste maps, town plans, ski schools, ski shops, kindergarten times, mountain guides weather reports and other information

Alpbach
www.alpbach.at
Tel: +43 (0)5 336 600-0

Alpe d'Huez
www.alpedhuez.com
Tel: +33 (0)4 76 80 44 41

Arosa
www.arosa.ch
Tel: +41 (0)81 378 7020

Bad Gastein
www.badgastein.at
Tel: +43 (0)64 32 33 93-560

Bourg Saint Maurice
www.lesarcs.com
Tel: +33 (0)4 79 07 12 57

Breuil Cervinia
www.montecervino.it
Tel: +39 0166 949 136

Briançon
www.briancon.com
Tel: +33 (0)4 92 21 08 50

Chamonix Valley
www.chamonix.net
Tel: +33 (0)4 50 54 60 71

Champoluc
www.ayas-champoluc.com
Tel: +39 0125 307 113

Château d'Oex
www.chateau-doex.ch
Tel: +41 (0)26 924 25 25

Cogne
www.cogne.org
Tel: +39 0165 74040

Cortina d'Ampezzo
www.cortina.dolomiti.com
Tel: +39 04 36 866252

Courchevel
www.courchevel.com
Tel: +33 (0)4 79 08 00 29

Courmayeur
www.courmayeur.net
Tel: +39 0165 842 060

Crans-Montana
www.cransmontana.ch
Tel: +41 (0)27 485 0404

Davos
www.davos.ch
Tel: +41 (0)81 415 21 21

Flims-Laax
www.laax.ch
Tel: +41 (0)81 920 92 00

Grindelwald
www.grindelwald.ch
Tel: +41 (0)33 854 12 12

Photo above Allys Williams

Resort Tourist offices

Gstaad
www.gstaad.ch
Tel: +41 (0)33 748 8181

Innsbruck
www.innsbruck-tourism.at
Tel: +43 (0)51 259 850

Ischgl
www.ischgl.com
Tel: +43 (0)54 44 5266-0

Kandersteg
www.kandersteg.ch
Tel: +41 (0)33 675 80 81

Kaprun
www.kaprun.at
Tel: +43 (0)65 478 64 30

Kitzbuhel
www.kitzbuehel.com
Tel: +43 (0)5356 621 55-0

Klosters
www.klosters.ch
Tel: +41 (0)81 410 20 20

La Clusaz
www.laclusaz.com
Tel: +33 (0)4 50 32 65 0

Les Arcs/La Plagne
www.la-plagne.com
Tel: +33 (0)4 79 09 79 79

La Grave
www.la-grave.com
Tel: +33 (0)4 76 79 90 05

La Thuile
www.lathuile.it
Tel: +39 0165 88 41 79

Le Grand Bornand
www.legrandbornand.com
Tel: +33 (0)4 50 02 78 00

Lech
www.lech-zeurs.at
Tel: +43 (0)5583 21 61-0

Les Contamines
www.lescontamines.com
Tel: +33 (0)4 50 47 01 58

Les Gets
www.lesgets.com
Tel: +33 (0)4 50 75 80 80

Madonna di Campiglio
www.campiglio.net
Tel: +39 04 65 44 20 00

Megève
www.megeve.com
Tel: +33 (0)4 50 21 27 28

Morzine
www.morzine-avoriaz.com
Tel: +33 (0)4 50 74 72 72

Mürren
www.muerren.ch
Tel: +41 (0)33 856 86 86

Obergurgl
www.obergurgl.com
Tel: +43 (0)52 56 64 66

Saas Fee
www.saas-fee.ch
Tel: +41 (0)27 958 18 58

Samoens
www.samoens.com
Tel: +33 (0)4 50 34 40 28

Sauze
D'Oulxwww.comune.sauzedoulx.to.it
Tel: +39 0122 850 380

Serre Chevalier
www.serre-chevalier.com
Tel: +33 (0)92 24 98 98

St Anton
www.stantonamarlberg.com
Tel: +43 (0)5446 2269-0

St Mortiz
www.stmoritz.ch
Tel: +41 (0)81 837 33 33

Ste Foy Tarentaise
www.saintefoy.net
Tel: +33 (0)4 79 06 95 19

Val d'Isère
www.valdisere.com
Tel: +33 (0)4 79 06 06 60

Valmorel
www.valmorel.com
Tel: +33 (0)4 79 09 85 55

Verbier
www.verbier.ch
Tel: +41 (0)27 775 38 88

Villars
www.villars.ch
Tel: +41 (0)24 495 32 32

Wengen
www.wengen-muerren.ch
Tel: +41 (0)33 855 14 14

Zell am See
www.zellamsee.at
Tel: +43 (0)6 542 77 00

Zermatt
www.zermatt.ch
Tel: +41 (0)27 966 81 00

UK information
Austrian Tourist Office
P. O. Box 2363, London, W1A 2QB.
Tel: 0207 629 0461

Italian Tourist Office
1 Princes Street, London W1R 8AY.
Tel: 0207 408 1254

Swiss Tourism
Swiss Centre 10 Wardour Street,
London W1D 6QF.
Tel: 0207 292 1550

Maison de la France
178 Piccadilly, London W1J 9AL.
Tel: (09068) 244 123 (information
line; calls cost 60p per minute)

US information
Italian Tourist Office
630 Fifth Avenue, New York 10111.
Tel: 212 245 5618

Austrian Tourist Office
P. O. Box 1142, New York,
NY 10108 -1142.
Tel : 212 944 6880

French Tourist Office
444 Madison Avenue, 16th Floor,
NY 10022.
Tel : 212 838 7800

Switzerland Tourism, Swiss Center,
608 Fifth Avenue, NY 10020.
Tel 1800 100 200 30

photo opposite Mike Richardson

The lack of fresh fruit and vegetables over the long winters has long been a major influence on mountain recipes. Traditionally, farmers would take their livestock to the high pastures in summer, during this time the lush grass on the lower slopes would be cut to make hay. In October, before the first snowfall, they would bring the animals back down and move them into the tightly-knit villages. Livestock would be herded into a barn, often below the living quarters, helping keep the farmer and his family warm. During this time the small vegetable garden would be under snow and the fruit trees bare; the family lived off yogurts, cheeses, grains, dried meats, preserved fruit, oats, potatoes and honey. From these basic ingredients the now world-famous 'muesli' and 'fondue' emerged – along with a few specialties they kept to themselves. Here are the recipes for four.

Salade de Chèvre Chaud
(Hot Goats Cheese Salad)
This classic Savoyard starter must be one of the simplest and most popular dishes in the region and is served at almost every mountain restaurant in the French Alps. The classic recipe has been changed to add more of a Savoyard flavour.

Serves 4

Mixed leaf salad
Goats cheese
Punnet of blueberries
Speck (or Parma ham)
Farmhouse bread
Light dressing

Place a handful of torn-up mixed leaves onto four plates. Bake the goats cheese at 150C for 5-10 minutes until the outside starts to melt. Remove, cut into three slices and place on each salad. Gently split 10-15 blueberries between the thumb and index finger and sprinkle over. Tear the speck into long thin strips and place evenly on the top. Drizzle a little balsamic vinegar and extra virgin olive oil. Season and serve with chunks of farmhouse bread.

photo opposite Manoir de Bellecombe, no. 60

Zuppa Con Fungi e Canederli
(Chanterelle Soup with Dumplings)
This heartier winter entrée is
southern Tyrolean - an Alto Adige
recipe with a strong Austrian
influence. The dumplings may be
varied but are usually based on
stale breadcrumbs and egg. Here
they accompany chanterelles in a
light broth.

Serves 4
150g freshly picked chanterelle
mushrooms
1 small shallot, finely chopped
30g butter
1.5 litres chicken stock
small bunch of chives

For the dumplings:
150g fresh white breadcrumbs
3 egg yolks
2 tablespoons of finely chopped
flat-leaf parsley
60g parmesan, grated
1 handful of lardons
(shreds of bacon)
salt and pepper

To make the dumplings, mix the
breadcrumbs with the egg yolks,
parsley, parmesan, lardons and
some salt and pepper. When pliable,
shape into balls the size of a small
walnut. For the soup, clean the
mushrooms and cut any large ones
in half. Fry the sliced shallot in
butter; as soon as it starts to
colour, add the chanterelles. Sauté
for five minutes, then add the stock
and bring to the boil. Add the
dumplings to the boiling soup.
Simmer for five minutes, then
sprinkle with the chopped chives
and serve.

photo opposite www.paulgroomphotography.com

Tartiflette
Another Savoyard specialty.
A winter meal with more emphasis
on heartiness than presentation.

Serves 6

1.2kg potatoes
200g lardons (shreds of bacon)
1 onion
1 Reblochon cheese
2 tablespoons crème fraîche
35cl Apremont
(Savoyard dry white wine)

Peel the potatoes and boil until soft.
Remove from heat, drain and place
to one side.

Dice the onion and fry in a little
olive oil over a medium heat. Add
the lardons. Heavily butter an oven
dish, and line it with half the
lardons and onions. Cut the still-
warm potatoes into slices and place
on top. Add the rest of the onions,
and cover with the crème fraîche.
Slice the Reblochon into two so you
have two thin, circular pieces. Pour
over a glass of wine and place the
cheese on top. Pop into a very hot
oven (250C) until the cheese melts
and forms a crust. Serve piping hot.

Photo above Manoir de Bellecombe, no. 60

Apfelstrudel
Finish off with a delicious warm
Austrian apple cake. The dough must
be rolled out very thinly (or buy
frozen filo pastry).

Serves 4

For the dough :
150g bread flour
Pinch of salt
1 tablespoon vegetable oil
Glass of lukewarm water

For the filling:
1kg apples (Golden Delicious)
75g granulated sugar
1 tablespoon dark rum
75g raisins
Pinch of ground cinnamon
1 lemon (juice and zest)

For the buttered breadcrumbs:
150g unsalted butter
150g breadcrumbs

Knead flour, salt, oil and water into
a medium-firm dough. Divide into
two small round loaves, brush each
loaf with melted butter and let rest
for one hour. Peel, core and slice
apples. Mix in the sugar, raisins,
lemon zest, lemon juice, rum and
cinnamon and blend well. Roll the
dough loaves with a rolling pin, then
place the stretched dough onto a
sheet of baking paper. Coat two-
thirds of the sheet with buttered
breadcrumbs, and spread the apple
mix over the remaining third. Tear
off edges and shape the strudel into
a roll by lifting the baking paper.
Place strudel on a buttered baking
sheet and brush with melted butter.
Bake for 30-60 minutes at 180C to
200C.

Photo above Berghotel Tirol, no. 135

Fragile Earth series

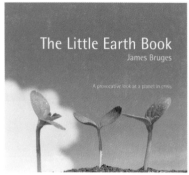

The Little Earth Book
Edition 4, £6.99
By James Bruges

A little book that has proved both hugely popular – and provocative. This new edition has chapters on Islam, Climate Change and The Tyranny of Corporations.

The Little Food Book
Edition 1, £6.99
By Craig Sams, Chairman of the Soil Association

An explosive account of the food we eat today. Never have we been at such risk - from our food. This book will help understand what's at stake.

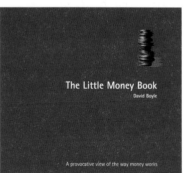

The Little Money Book
Edition 1, £6.99
By David Boyle, an associate of the New Economics Foundation

This pithy, wry little guide will tell you where money comes from, what it means, what it's doing to the planet and what we might be able to do about it.

www.fragile-earth.com

Six Days

Celebrating the triumph of creativity over adversity.

An inspiring and heart-rending story of the making of the stained glass 'Creation' window at Chester Cathedral by a woman battling with debilitating Parkinson's disease.

"Within a few seconds, the tears were running down my cheeks. The window was one of the most beautiful things I had ever seen. It is a tour-de force, playing with light like no other window ..."
Anthropologist Hugh Brody

In 1983, Ros Grimshaw, a distinguished designer, artist and creator of stained glass windows, was diagnosed with Parkinson's disease. Refusing to allow her illness to prevent her from working, Ros became even more adept at her craft, and in 2000 won the commission to design and make the 'Creation' Stained Glass Window for Chester Cathedral.

Six Days traces the evolution of the window from the first sketches to its final, glorious completion as a rare and wonderful tribute to Life itself: for each of the six 'days' of Creation recounted in Genesis, there is a scene below that is relevant to the world of today and tomorrow.

Heart-rending extracts from Ros's diary capture the personal struggle involved. Superb photography captures the luminescence of the stunning stained glass, while the story weaves together essays, poems, and moving contributions from Ros's partner, Patrick Costeloe.

Available from Alastair Sawday Publishing £12.99

Order Form

All these books are available in major bookshops or you may order them direct.
Post and packaging are FREE within the UK.

British Hotels, Inns & Other Places	£13.99
Bed & Breakfast for Garden Lovers	£14.99
British Holiday Homes	£9.99
Pubs & Inns of England & Wales	£13.99
London	£9.99
British Bed & Breakfast	£14.99
French Bed & Breakfast	£15.99
French Hotels, Châteaux & Inns	£13.99
French Holiday Homes	£11.99
Paris Hotels	£9.99
Ireland	£12.99
Spain	£13.99
Portugal	£8.99
Italy	£12.99
Mountains of Europe	£9.99
Europe with courses & activities	£12.99
India	£10.99
Morocco	£10.99
The Little Earth Book	£6.99
The Little Food Book	£6.99
The Little Money Book	£6.99
Six Days	£12.99

Please make cheques payable to Alastair Sawday Publishing. Total £ _____

Please send cheques to: Alastair Sawday Publishing, The Home Farm Stables,
Barrow Gurney, Bristol BS48 3RW. For credit card orders call 01275 464891 or
order directly from our web site www.specialplacestostay.com

Title   First name   Surname

Address

Postcode   Tel

SKI1

If you do not wish to receive mail from other like-minded companies, please tick here ☐
If you would prefer not to receive information about special offers on our books, please tick here ☐

Report Form

If you have any comments on entries in this guide, please let us have them.
If you have a favourite house, hotel, inn or other new discovery, please let us
know about it. You can e-mail info@sawdays.co.uk, too.

Existing entry:

Book title: _____

Entry no: _____ Edition no: _____

New recommendation:

Country: _____

Property name: _____

Address: _____

_____

_____

_____

Tel: _____

Comments: Report:

_____

_____

_____

_____

_____

_____

_____

Your name: _____

Address: _____

_____

_____

Tel: _____

Please send completed form to ASP, The Home Farm Stables,
Barrow Gurney, Bristol BS48 3RW or go to
www.specialplacestostay.com and click on 'contact'. Thank you.

Quick reference indices

Rooms for €100 or less
These places have a double or a twin room for two for €100 or under (or equivalent) per night. Check when booking.

Austria
Tirol 8 • 10 • 11 • 12 • 14 • 15 • 18 • 19
Salzburg 21 • 22

France
Rhône Valley-Alps 23 • 25 • 31 • 32 • 35 • 36 • 38 • 41 • 43 • 44 • 48 • 49 • 50 • 51 • 53 • 54 • 55 • 58 • 59 • 60 • 62 • 65 • 66 • 68 • 69 • 70 • 71
Provence-Alps-Riviera 67 • 72 • 75 • 76

Switzerland
Vaud 77 • 79 • 80
Bernese Oberland 84
Valais 90 • 91
Graubunden 95 • 97 • 98

Italy
Valle d'Aosta 104 • 105 • 107 • 108 • 109 • 110 • 111 • 112 • 114 • 120 • 121 • 123 • 125

Trentino-Alto Adige 128 • 129 • 131 • 133
Veneto 136 • 137

Singles for under €50
These places have rooms for singles for £50 or under per night.

Austria
Tirol 8 • 10 • 14 • 18 • 19

France
Rhône Valley-Alps 31 • 48 • 51 • 55 • 60 • 65 • 66
Provence-Alps-Riviera 72 • 73 • 74 • 75

Italy
Valle d'Aosta 104 • 108 • 109 • 114 • 120 • 124 • 125
Trentino-Alto Adige 128 • 129 • 133

Child Friendly Places
These owners welcome children.

Austria
Vorarlberg 1 • 2 • 3 • 4 • 5
Tirol 7 • 8 • 9 • 10 • 11 • 12 • 13 • 14 • 15 • 18 • 19
Salzburg 20 • 21

France
Rhône Valley-Alps 23 • 24 • 25 • 26 • 27 • 28 • 29 • 31 • 33 • 34 • 36 • 37 • 38 • 39 • 40 • 42 • 43 • 45 • 47 • 48 • 50 • 51 • 52 • 53 • 54 • 56 • 57 • 58 • 59 • 62 • 63 • 65 • 66 • 69 • 70

Photo opposite Allys Williams

Pet-Friendly Places
These owners welcome pets.

Photo opposite Tim Brook

Limited Mobility
Need a ground-floor bedroom and
bathroom? Try these.

Quick reference indices

Switzerland
Bernese Oberland 83 • 84 • 85 • 88
Valais 91
Graubunden 100

Italy
Valle d'Aosta 104 • 105 • 106 • 107
• 113 • 117 • 121 • 123
Trentino-Alto Adige 132 • 134 • 135
Veneto 136

Wheelchair accessible
If you need places which are
wheelchair-accessible, contact these
places.

Austria
Tirol 19

France
Rhône Valley-Alps 25 • 49 • 53

Switzerland
Bernese Oberland 83 • 85

Italy
Valle d'Aosta 104 • 106 • 107 • 113
• 118 • 121 • 123
Trentino-Alto Adige 132 • 133

One hour or less from the airport
These places are within easy reach
of major airports.

Austria

Vorarlberg 6
Tirol 10 • 11 • 12 • 13 • 15 • 16 • 18
Salzburg 20 • 22

France
Rhône Valley-Alps 29 • 32 • 33 • 34
• 35 • 36 • 39 • 40 • 41 • 42 • 43
• 44 • 45 • 46 • 49 • 51 • 52

Italy
Trentino-Alto Adige 128

B&B
These places provide Bed and
Breakfast.

Austria
Tirol 12 • 14 • 17
Salzburg 22

France
Rhône Valley-Alps 25 • 35 • 36 • 38
• 43 • 44 • 48 • 51 • 54 • 55 • 56
• 58 • 59 • 60 • 62 • 66 • 68 • 69
• 70
Provence-Alps-Riviera 67 • 72 • 75
• 76

Photo opposite Nick Woodford

Switzerland
Vaud 77 • 80
Bernese Oberland 84

Italy
Valle d'Aosta 108 • 109 • 111 • 114
• 116 • 120
Trentino-Alto Adige 129
Veneto 136

50m from piste
Want to be close to the piste? Try these.

Austria
Vorarlberg 1 • 3 • 5
Tirol 17 • 18 • 19

France
Rhône Valley-Alps 25 • 26 • 28 • 29
• 30 • 37 • 47 • 51 • 52 • 56 • 57

Photo above Nick Woodford

• 61 • 64

Switzerland
Bernese Oberland 87
Graubunden 96 • 99

Italy
Valle d'Aosta 115 • 125

Catered Chalets
These places are catered.

Austria
Vorarlberg 4

France
Rhône Valley-Alps 23 • 24 • 27 • 28
• 39 • 41 • 52 • 57 • 65

Switzerland
Valais 93

Italy
Trentino-Alto Adige 126

Self-catering
Fancy whipping up a strundel yourself? Try these places.

Austria
Tirol 8 • 18

France
Rhône Valley-Alps 23 • 27 • 30 • 33
• 34 • 39 • 40 • 41 • 47 • 52 • 57
• 63 • 65

Switzerland
Valais 93

Index by property name

Index by place name

Photo opposite Tim Brook

How to use this book

① **Rhône Valley-Alps :** Portes du Soleil **②**

La Ferme de Nant
La Ville du Nant, 74360 La Chapelle d'Abondance, Haute-Savoie, France

③ Upstairs is chic and contemporary, downstairs traditional. Susie and Steve have transformed the 1789 farmhouse into a superb chalet that's fully catered in winter. Floor-to-ceiling windows opening to a sunny balcony pull in the views. The open-plan kitchen/living/dining area is vast, with doors off to the bedrooms. Floors are wooden and gleaming, halogen spots illuminate white walls, there's a mix of Savoyard and modern and a giant pop art portrait to add a sparkle. From the first floor you descend the stairs – past a fascinating collection of old wooden sledges that came with the house – to the more traditionally furnished ground floor. This is a delightfully cosy space with an open fireplace in the middle, good new sofas and beautiful country-antique dining room table and chairs. A trap-door leads to a cellar packed with DVDs, yours for winter evenings; the slopey garden has been reshaped to make way for a good-sized, heated pool, open from March. In winter the owners, who live on the top floor with their labrador, can drive you to the pistes. Susie also owns a horse – the riding is wonderful.

rooms	6 doubles/twins. Extra beds.	**④**
price	B&B €100. Self-catering per week: one floor €1,200; two floors €2,250. Winter: €785-€1,125 p.p. p.w.	**⑤**
meals	Dinner €22. Self-catering June-August. Catered in winter.	**⑥**
closed	May & October-November.	**⑦**
directions	D22 for Chatel; thro' La Chapelle, then left at sign for La Croix. Chalet on 3nd bend.	**⑧**

Self-catering/Catered/B&B **⑨**

piste or lift	1km	**⑩**
cross-country trail	1.5km	
lift for bikes	2km	
village centre	1.5km	

	Susie Ward
tel	+44 (0)1872 553055
fax	+44 (0)450 734087
e-mail	susie@susieward.com
web	www.susieward.com

⑫ Map 1 Entry 23

⑪

explanation

1 region & **2** ski region

---

3 write up

Write-up, written by us.

---

4 rooms

Assume most but not all rooms are en suite; some will have separate or shared bath/shower rooms.

---

5 price

The price shown is for one night B&B for two people sharing a room. Half-board prices are per person. Catered/self-catered prices are per chalet per week, unless stated otherwise. A price range incorporates room/seasonal differences.

---

6 meals

Prices are per person. If breakfast isn't included we give the price. All other meals must be booked in advance.

---

7 closed

When given in months, this means for the whole of the named months and the time in between.

---

8 directions

Use as a guide and travel with a good map; the owner can give more details.

---

9 type of place

B&B, hotel, catered or self-catered chalet. (Guesthouses, inns and restaurants with rooms come under 'B&B' or 'Hotel').

---

10 distance

To nearest piste or lift, cross-country trail, lift for bikes and village centre (in metres and kilometres).

---

11 symbols

see the last page of the book for a fuller explanation:

&#x267F;	wheelchair facilities		english spoken
👤	easily accessible bedrooms	🍎	good vegetarian dinner options
👶	all children welcome	🐕	guests' pets welcome
✗	no smoking anywhere	🐈	owners pets live here
💳	credit cards accepted	🏊	pool
		🚲	bikes on the premises
		🎾	tennis on the premises

---

12 map & entry numbers

Map number; entry number.

www.specialplacestostay.com

Britain • France • India • Ireland • Italy • Morocco • Portugal • Spain... all in one place!

On the unfathomable and often unnavigable sea of online accommodation pages, those who have discovered www.specialplacestostay.com have found it to be an island of reliability. Not only will you find a database full of trustworthy, up-to-date information about all of our Special Places to Stay, but also:

- Links to the web sites of all of the places in the series
- Colourful, clickable, interactive maps to help you find the right place
- The opportunity to make most bookings by e-mail – even if you don't have e-mail yourself
- Online purchasing of our books, securely and cheaply
- Regular, exclusive special offers on books
- The latest news about future editions and future titles
- Special offers and news from our owners

The site is constantly evolving and is frequently updated with news and special features that won't appear anywhere else but in our window on the worldwide web.

Russell Wilkinson, Web Site Manager
website@specialplacestostay.com

If you'd like to receive news and updates about our books by e-mail, send a message to
newsletter@specialplacestostay.com